Indoor Gardening
made easy

Indoor Gardening
made easy

Gay Hellyer

Hamlyn
London·New York·Sydney·Toronto

Acknowledgements
The publishers would like to thank
Pat Brindley, John Cowley, John
Howard and Philip James for the
photographs used in this book and
Q-Cloche Ltd. for the loan of the table
conservatory illustrated on page 11.

First published in 1976 by The Hamlyn Publishing Group Ltd.,
London · New York · Sydney · Toronto
Astronaut House, Feltham, Middlesex, England
Copyright © The Hamlyn Group Ltd., 1976

ISBN 0 600 34884 9

Printed and bound by Smeets, Holland

Filmset in England by Siviter Smith & Co. Ltd.,
Birmingham
Set in 10 on 11pt Plantin

Contents

Introduction

Anybody living in a house, flat or apartment could grow all the plants mentioned in this book without recourse to sunroom, garden, greenhouse or frame. People used to gardens do not necessarily have a great advantage over the newcomer when growing house plants, for conditions indoors are very different, and some gardeners find it hard to remember how completely dependent on their care a house plant is. If there is no greenhouse, frame or sunroom available to act as a hospital after your neglect or excess of zeal the only alternative is to learn how to prevent the plant from getting out of condition in the first place.

I have assumed that the house plants will have reached you through a shop, nursery or friend, and not that you have the right light conditions or space to raise them yourself from seeds or cuttings, though many can easily be raised by amateurs.

Plants coming from florists will occasionally have been chilled, simply because florists are used to keeping their cut flowers cool; so avoid high–temperature lovers when buying from a florist. In department stores, which buy in large quantities for distribution among their branches, it is important to be very selective: plants may have been roughly handled, too young to stand the journey, badly watered or left in a polluted atmosphere because the assistants lack the necessary training or have no control over public smoking or the aerosols used to 'purify' the air in the shop. Plants from garden centres and nurseries, provided these are properly run, should have suffered none of these checks. The specialist nurseries will have the larger selection, but too wide a choice may be confusing to a beginner.

Plants from friends' collections are fine in theory, but beware of introducing pests. The specialist nurseries, which also supply most of the garden centres and florists' shops, should spray their plants regularly, but even they can miss the odd insect. Friends may not even know what to look for, and if the new owner does not either the pests may have spread to all his other plants before he realizes. If a start can be made with clean plants the few insects that come in through the window are easily controlled.

I have not included many bulbs because the ones needing indoor temperatures are not easy to obtain dry, let alone about to bloom, and many are more decorative cut than when growing. Nerines, vallotas, and hymenocallis are good examples: they do not last long enough to justify keeping the pot for the rest of the year.

I have only included the two most readily available orchids. There are plenty more that are no harder to keep through their flowering period, and many last for a long time in flower, but they are only obtainable from specialists. I have included just two cacti, both from high–humidity areas, because although the dry air of centrally heated houses suits most cacti, many of them also need much more sun than penetrates houses, and extra lighting is costly if used regularly. Added to which—and this is a purely personal feeling—I do not think cacti mix easily with other house plants, though I am prepared to admit that many have intriguing shapes which may suit the architecture of a house.

I have tried to explain how room conditions differ from natural ones; perhaps I should also say that the greenhouse conditions in which most house plants have been raised will be

different again, and at the time of purchase are what the plant will have been in. The first few days of acclimatizing it to your house may make all the difference to success. Give the plant the very best you have and gradually wean it to something less ideal if you have to.

I have also explained *why* plants need a recommended treatment, because I like to know why I am doing anything, but it is not necessary for you to know this and if you are prepared to follow the instructions blindly you will get just as good results!

The time will come in the life of any house plant when it has outgrown its space or is no longer ornamental. Be prepared to discard it. If it was costly to buy, someone with more room who is able to use it for cuttings or willing to give it shelter while in its resting period can often be found. Ask children; they usually know someone who will give it a home. Cut your own losses whenever it is at all possible.

Left to right: *Pteris cretica albo-lineata, Dieffenbachia arvida exotica, Solanum capsicastrum* and *Plectranthus australis,* a trailing green-foliaged plant easily grown

Making house plants happy

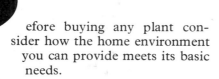

Before buying any plant consider how the home environment you can provide meets its basic needs.

House Conditions

Temperature.
No matter in what part of the world men build houses they try to make the conditions inside them tolerable, either by keeping the interior warmer than the air outside, or by cooling it, closing windows and shutters by day to trap the cooler night air and keep the day temperature down. What the actual tolerable temperature is (in degrees) depends more on the customs of the inhabitants than on any scientific criteria.

Plants in all areas are used to being cooler at night than by day; they do not need the constant temperature of a thermostatically controlled room, but they will acclimatize to it. What they will not put up with is a temperature that falls below a certain minimum. It is not much use keeping the plant at that minimum all the time; the temperature needs to rise above it at some part of the day or the plant will not actively grow. In nature some plants have to survive very big changes in temperature between day and night, but in compensation most get bright sun to ripen their growth. In the poor light of houses the fall should not be much over 5°c (10°F). Whatever the actual temperature is in the house it will vary to suit the human beings and their way of life, and it is rarely that the plants get much consideration. Many can be acclimatized to your temperature routine if you do this gradually, but the others you will have to forego. Buy new plants in the spring or early summer when conditions are less likely to be extremely different inside and out, for then there are fewer draughts, and your temperatures will not be too different from those where the plant was grown.

Light
To have a roof over your head necessarily cuts off some sunlight. The amount shut out is not readily appreciated for human eyes adapt very quickly and with less strain to the shadows than to bright light. It is only by comparing photographic light meter readings taken in and out of doors, in the direct light of a window and the permanent shadows of a corner of a room where no direct sunshine ever falls, that most people can get any idea of how much light a plant is deprived when it is brought indoors. Light is essential for plants, which use their chlorophyll (green pigment) to trap some of the energy of light to build up their very diverse structures. Without light they cannot even use the food given them in their potting mix. Fortunately some plants can work in a comparatively low light intensity. Those which are not getting enough may show it by making elongated growth with thin leaves on floppy stems; it is lack of enough light which makes it necessary to stake hyacinths in bowls indoors while the same variety in beds outside stand firmly upright on stems which are shorter and stiffer.

Even plants on a sill inside a window get less light than if they were standing on the outer ledge and in both cases they receive far less than where the light can come freely from all sides. Double glazing or a Wardian case shuts off even more light, and overhanging eaves and shutters make things still worse. The further away from the window the poorer the light.

Water

Whatever else you do to your house plants it is esstential to give them water, sometimes lime–free water (which is not always available from the tap), and their requirements will be found to vary enormously, not only between one kind of plant and another but between an actively growing plant and one in its resting stage or when it is kept near its minimum temperature, and between one in the direct rays of the sun and another of the same kind in diffuse light.

Just as much as needing water in the soil at their roots, plants also need a moist atmosphere around their leaves, usually much moister than that in which people would choose to live. The warmer the air the more water vapour it can hold and therefore the more it takes from the leaves of plants. They can lose water to the air faster than their roots are able to replace it from the soil water, and their leaves may droop or the edges may appear burnt because the thin tissues there have become desiccated and dead.

The Range of Plants that can be Grown Indoors

So plants indoors are likely to be kept in a different temperature, differing not only from that of their native habitat but also from that of the greenhouse in which they were raised, with a lower light intensity and without their optimum humidity or rainfall. Therefore if you do not wish to alter radically the conditions in your home you will have to look out for plants likely to tolerate them. These are unlikely to be plants from mountains (wrong temperature range), from sunbaked deserts and prairies (wrong light intensities), or from stream sides (wrong water requirements).

Temperaturewise they will tend to be plants from sub–tropical parts which do not mind if occasionally the air heats up to 21°C (70°F) (or do you live a very Spartan life?). Lightwise they can be plants from within forests where the light intensity is greatly reduced by the tree canopy so that they are used to living in dappled light or in shade. As far as water is concerned you may think that succulents from dry areas will be less demanding. They often will withstand a measure of neglect that would kill less tough plants, but even they need adequate water during their growing season and they are used to high light intensities. Arguing thus, you end up with the aspidistra and sansevieria!

The majority of house plants probably do come from sub–tropical forest areas and include the bromeliads, the peperomias and lots of ferns and climbers such as monstera. Most are not grown for flowers but for fine foliage, variegated forms frequently being the most prized.

But you cannot always tell and some plants from unlikely habitats make good house plants, for example the Australian tree *Grevillea robusta*. People are constantly collecting new kinds, experimenting with unlikely ones, breeding for special features, looking for new variants of old favourites. So much so that many of the plants we are growing today were neither known nor thought of as house plants 20 years ago, and more will be here as the years go by. I was reared on aspidistra, the Norfolk Island pine and the potted palm, with the occasional fern to test my skill.

Actually there are many micro–climates in most houses, even before making any special arrangements, so a wide range can be accommodated. Halls and passages are often darker and cooler than other parts and sometimes subject to sudden draughts; bathrooms and kitchens often have a higher humidity; some windows may face the sun, others rarely receive any; some are large, warming up or cooling the air rapidly, others are draughty. Some rooms are warm all the time, others barely heated for part of the day; some may have a smoky fire or smoking humans or the air may be polluted by a main road or factory, or by the use of aerosols to kill flies. There are plants which will survive or enjoy all these conditions, short of actual freezing, though many would do better with somewhat more congenial surroundings.

Improving Conditions

The easiest way to obtain the ideal plant climate without altering your own living conditions is to build it into a plant cabinet, but unless you are very enthusiastic or prepared to look upon it as a piece of furniture—such as a room divider—you will probably consider it too costly. Plant cabinets need to be wired up to a suitable electric point by a skilled electrician for they are warmed, heated and lit in damp surroundings.

Simpler micro–climates are obtainable in bottle gardens, plastic domes (the tops of which lift off for easy maintenance), Wardian cases (like small greenhouses for use in bay windows) or disused aquarium tanks, with or without glass lids. But all these limit you to small plants and with the exception of the plant cabinet they may need additional lighting placed near by. This should come on regularly, even when you are not there; but that is a counsel of perfection.

Bottle gardens

These are best made in carboys, but smaller bottles can be used for single plants. The plant mix should be peat based and contain some charcoal. It must be just moist, not soggy, and be funnelled in carefully to avoid messing up the sides. The plants must be small, slow growing and all needing the same temperature. They have to be planted by ingenious means, such as using canes to which tablespoons and forks have been fixed for making holes, and an old–fashioned wooden cotton reel or other wooden block to act as a soil firmer around the plant. It is best to set the plants out on a comparable area outside the bottle so that you know just where each has to go, for it is difficult to have second thoughts later.

The only maintenance required, besides watering twice a year if you keep the top closed, or every few months if open, is to remove any piece of plant that dies, before it has time to rot and infect the others. Flowering plants are never used in bottles for this reason. Any plant liable to overrun others may have to be cut off with a sharp knife or razor blade and the pieces hauled out, but this rarely happens because the plants grow so slowly. They take in carbon dioxide from the air during the day and use

it to grow, giving off oxygen in the process. Then when there is no more light some of the oxygen is taken up by the plants when breathing, and so carbon dioxide is excreted into the air. These gaseous exchanges are in fine balance and plants in bottles or other closed or nearly closed structures do not grow in weight to any great extent, which is just as well or the beds would have to be remade more frequently than once in three years (the average life of a bottle garden). In stoppered bottles the sides mist up with the condensed water, but they are otherwise quite satisfactory.

Plastic domes

These have the advantage over glass carboys that they let in more light and have a removable top, which

greatly aids any maintenance. They take similar plants and can be left unattended in the same way as a bottle.

Wardian cases

Wardian cases are like small greenhouses, usually metal framed and with a roof that opens or can be removed for easy maintenance. They often have some means of allowing excess water to drain away, which does not exist in bottles and domes. For this reason they are more suitable for plants where a high water supply is linked with good drainage and high humidity. An alternative is to use a discarded fish or aquarium tank on top of which loose sheets of glass can be laid, or for which a permanent lid can be made. The lid or sheets can be removed when using the tank to

A plastic dome provides a pleasing alternative to a bottle garden. Included in this planting are *Neanthe bella* and *Cryptanthus bivittatus*

Top right
A simple terrarium constructed in a fish tank

Bottom right
This 'Table Conservatory' can be used to revive flagging house plants or as a permanent home for more tender subjects

acclimatize to room conditions a plant formerly kept in a sealed container. They make good 'hospitals' for plants recovering from the shock of too big a temperature change, too much or too little water, too drying air or draughty conditions.

Plant cabinets
Plant cabinets which possess artificial lighting, watering and heating are expensive, but they do allow you to grow not only most of the easy house plants (if not too big) but also many too difficult to manage easily without additional protection. Ideally the cabinet should be on castors, allowing it to be adapted to the various other uses of the room and placed in positions where the plants can be viewed from both sides.

Changing Your Own Conditions

Making an effort to change your own
conditions to suit your plants is
another thing entirely. If your home
is centrally heated, try to keep the
difference between day and night
temperatures around 10°C (20°F). If
the heating only goes up ready for
your return from work in the evening,
try to ensure that the lower day temperature is still within the plant's
range. It does not matter if the greater
heat is by night rather than by day
provided there is enough light for the
plant at the warmer time.

Any plant which enjoys a cooler
atmosphere than most of your rooms
may perhaps be accommodated in a
hall or passage, or even moved to a
room which is unoccupied for much
of the year.

Artificial lighting

The level of daylight and artificial
light varies greatly from house to
house and room to room, but it is
possible to grow plants needing a
higher level of light than natural daylight can provide indoors by giving
them additional lighting artificially.
(You can make use of this light
yourself—it need not be entirely an
extra.) A lamp will also add to the

heat, which may or may not be an
advantage.

The most effective and coolest
artificial aids are mercury fluorescent
reflector lamps, either tubes or bulbs.
These can be switched on to intensify
the daylight or can be turned on during the hours of darkness to add to
the day length at either end of the
natural day. Which suits the plant
best will depend on the latitude in
which it grows naturally, for plants
from tropical regions have days which
are very similar in length to the
nights.

Some plants are super–sensitive
about their day length (or, more cor-
rectly, their night length) and refuse
to make flower buds (e.g. schlumbergera) or colour their bracts (e.g. poin-
settia) if the night length is curtailed
below about 13 hours. So you have
the choice of buying such a plant in
bud and discarding it after flowering
or of adjusting the night length to suit
it, when it will probably make more
buds immediately and certainly the
following year. This may mean putting it in a room where the light will
not be switched on at all during the
evening, for even a short break is
enough to upset this delicate control.
The alternative of covering the plant
nightly along with the budgerigar is
not as easy as it sounds, for it has
to be done very accurately. Growers
of 'all–the–year–round' chrysanthemums regularly black out their plants
once they have reached the height
which will look best in a pot. This
height has been obtained by the use
of dwarfing chemicals. This does not
concern the house plant enthusiast,
for nobody is likely to want to grow
on a chrysanthemum plant once it has
flowered, but it explains why you can
buy them at any season, why the production of such plants is best left to
specialists and why, if your cast–off
plant is planted in a garden, it will
produce chrysanthemum plants of a
different height flowering at a different time altogether.

There are other plants, such as
fuchsias, which need a short night for
bud production. These do not make
good house plants since they need
very good light to keep flowering and
resent any movement of the pot,
which causes them to drop their
flowers. Very few house plants are of
this type for these are plants from the
temperate areas.

If it is necessary to increase lighting
to bring a plant into flower the best
lamp to use is a tungsten filament type
which gives out a lot of heat. The
grower would automatically switch
this on for ½ to 1 hour in the middle
of the night. But you can give the
extra light any time to suit yourself
so long as it breaks up the hours of

darkness. Just move in on the plant and use the light for yourself as well.

The green and yellow pigments of leaves become deeper in colour in good light, so almost all variegated leaves benefit by being in good diffuse light, even if they will grow in deep shade, because the extra light sharpens the colour contrast. Give them all a turn nearer the window and use the sun lovers to keep the brightest light off the furnishings. Remember to turn the pots fairly regularly; quick–growing subjects like hyacinths need a quarter turn per day, to keep them from growing one–sidedly towards the source of light.

Air

Most plants do perfectly well without a change of air such as human beings prefer, and though there are a few which seem to appreciate free movement of air there are very few which will tolerate draughts. Draughts are not merely quick–moving streams of cold air coming through badly fitting sashes and under doors, they include also the stream of hot air blown from a fan heater or rising from a radiator, and the cooled air from an air conditioner. Moving air which is less humid than the air around the plant will dry the water from its leaves often more rapidly than the plant can replace it from the soil water, and so causes desiccation of the thin leaf tips or edges, which often go brown.

Many draughts can be cured and others can be circumvented by such simple means as putting plants on stands 30cm (1ft) off the floor or moving them in from the window or out of any direct stream of air.

Pollution

Some plants, especially thin–leaved ones (and all leaves grown indoors are relatively thinner than if grown in the open) are very susceptible to air pollutants such as tobacco smoke, motor car exhaust fumes, some cooking smells and especially fumes from badly adjusted paraffin (kerosene) stoves and the solvent in aerosols, including insecticidal ones. Others are intolerant of accumulated dust on their surface and need washing or spraying regularly. Do not be tempted to use a vacuum cleaner!

Bottom
Plants with variegated foliage may occasionally give rise to green shoots. These should be removed as soon as they are noticed

Opposite, top
The offshoots of *Chlorophytum comosum variegatum* can be individually layered into small pots and severed from the parent plant when they have become established, usually only a few weeks later

Opposite, bottom
Plants like this billbergia with several crowns can be divided and the resulting plants potted individually

Humidity

Water vapour in the air, which is called its humidity, can be kept where it is wanted (round the leaves) by putting plants in groups out of draughts, or by packing moist peat around pots in a trough, and can be improved by spraying the plants or misting the air around them. Misting is the best method for fragile leaves, especially those of ferns, which can become water–soaked, showing translucent spots which later turn black, if too heavily watered. Water trays add to the humidity generally, but the air of the room is best moistened by using a humidifier. There are several different kinds on the market.

The humidity of air in rooms heated by hot pipes or electricity compares badly with that in which a gas, open fire or paraffin heater is burning, because these all produce water as a by–product of combustion. Hot–air systems can be arranged to blow the warm air over water before it enters the rooms, so that it is no longer too dry. The worst place in the room for a plant will be immediately over a radiator where the hot air is rising and taking up water from anything moist, such as plant leaves, en route. At one time radiators were made with a water trough on top, but now they are so narrow it is not possible to stand a saucer of water on them and water can only be hung from the top in a suitable container.

But there is no sense in overdoing the humidity of the air. This would make it uncomfortable for human beings, so it is best to add extra water to the air just where it is needed. A single specimen plant can have its pot enclosed in an ornamental container with the space between packed with moist peat or sphagnum moss, and any plant in special need can be put into a Wardian case for a short spell, if not permanently.

Soil Mixtures

House plants are hardly ever grown in the type of soil you might expect to find in a garden, varied though that may be. They are almost always grown in special mixes, some based on loam, but many based on peat and almost all containing some peat. These mixes are sterile (that is, they do not contain soil pests or weed seeds) and are of known ingredients which enables them to be re–mixed time and again. They are usually put in bags small enough to carry home and use without mess, without waste and without having to store more than a few pounds if it is not all used at one time.

The peat–based mixes are very light in weight and are moist when

A plant pole provides an unusual and effective means of displaying house plants; particularly those with a trailing habit

you receive them. They are all very clean to work with but some are very difficult to re–wet if allowed to dry out. These peat mixes contain sufficient chemical fertilizer to last a plant in a greenhouse for six to eight weeks. Indoors, where plants grow more slowly, they may last even longer, but eventually feeding with fertilizer will be necessary (except where indicated) if only because in pots the proportion of soil to roots is so small.

Plants with much heavy top growth need a loam–based soil mix, not only to supply the greater quantity of food needed but also to support a cane better. Loam–based mixes do not leach their food into the drainage water as readily as peat mixes do. There are many loam–based mixtures, but the best known in Britain are those made to the John Innes Institute's formulations and called the John Innes Potting Composts. These are sold with three different strengths of fertilizer, and are sometimes also available with sulphur in place of superphosphate of lime for lime–hating plants. The potting composts are JIP.1 for slow growers, JIP.2 for most plants and JIP.3 for the vigorous ones. Comparable American soil mixtures are those developed at the University of California and known as U.C. composts.

Special peat mixes are made for bulbs and other plants growing in bowls which have no drainage holes. In addition to the peat they contain crushed charcoal and some form of lime, usually shell, also crushed. These absorb and neutralize the acids which form as a result of bacterial activity in waterlogged soils, preventing them from becoming sour, but this does not stop the soil spaces from filling up with water and drowning the roots, so exceptional care has to be given to watering plants in bowls. They must not be stood out in the rain—a method of watering which is not usually good for house plants as the rain is likely to be much colder than the soil in the pot, causing chilling.

Watering

Water can be poured on the surface of the soil, or be sprayed all over the plant. Alternatively the water can be supplied to the pots from below. The pot can be put into a bowl of water, or water be added to the plant saucer. When it is obvious that the water has been soaked up into the soil mix from below, any water left in the saucer must be removed. No plant should be left standing in water for longer than half an hour, or the soil nutrients will be washed out, the plant may be chilled and the roots drowned.

Another alternative is to stand the plant permanently on a tray covered with sand, pebbles or other aggregate or purpose–made absorbent white plastic felt cloth. This can then be flooded occasionally or the water level, which should be just below the surface of the aggregate, can be maintained by fitting up a feed system. This can be a large inverted bottle which lets the water out slowly as the tray dries. Plastic pots with peat mixes take up water well from such trays, but clay pots usually require fitting with a wick protruding through the drainage hole into the water.

Special double pots are also available which use a wick to soak up water from the outer reservoir and feed it to the plant in the inner container. They are invaluable for places like offices where plants often suffer from irregular watering.

Overhead watering is not easy indoors, for apart from the chances of ruining furniture and carpets with splashes it is difficult to assess how much of the water has reached the soil. Spraying is occasionally worth while if you have a big sink or a shower unit and wish to wash the foliage at the same time.

Watering from the spout of a can may dislodge the soil from around the neck of the plant if it rushes out too fast, so care is needed. Use a small can which you can control easily and which has a long slender spout that can be guided in between plants in a group without damage to foliage.

The water should never come straight from a cold tap, but should be at room temperature, or slightly above—up to 21°C (70°F). Enough should be given at a time so that it runs out of the drainage holes at the bottom of the pot. The frequency of watering will depend upon the plant's rate of growth; watering should always be much less frequent when a plant is near its minimum temperature. Most house plants suffer more from overwatering than underwatering.

Some plants are sufficiently lime hating to be upset by tap water. If it is available rain water is the best alternative, but it is rarely obtainable by flat dwellers, who may therefore have recourse to distilled water or to boiled water. But be warned. The distilled water sold by garages for topping up batteries usually contains acid, so get the genuine article which is sold for steam irons. Boiled water must be allowed to cool to room temperature before it is used. It will not be lime free, but the amount of soluble lime will be less, and even lime haters need some lime.

Most plants will stand underwatering better than overwatering, but if

Feed actively growing house plants regularly

peat mixes become too dry they do not always take up water readily, and it may be necessary to soak such a plant in a bowl of water, giving the peat time to become properly wet again. It is possible to check the condition of the soil by tapping the plant out of its pot, as in repotting, but this should only be done if you suspect things are not right with the roots. Soil mixes which become waterlogged very easily can be improved by the addition of extra grit or coarse sand to help drainage. Quick–draining composts usually need more frequent watering. Waterlogging may be caused by a blocked drainage hole or lack of coarse material in the base of a clay pot. Any plants I have found to be especially sensitive to watering irregularities are indicated as such in the text.

Feeding

Peat mixes contain food for a shorter time than loam–based ones, but most pot plants need feeding at some time, usually when making their most rapid growth. When the plant is a disposable, short stay one there is usually no need to feed at all unless the pot is obviously too small and full of roots, when one small feed may help

to prolong its flowering period.

Plants need a good mixed fertilizer, which should supply nitrogen, potash and phosphorus and occasionally some trace elements. Because very small amounts of the trace elements are needed it is wise to ring the changes on the fertilizer used so that the chances of any one trace element being absent or in excess is lessened. The fertilizer can be given as a powder or even as a pellet, but for house plants the best results are likely to be obtained by using a solution made up either as directed by the manufacturer or in a lesser concentration. Always err on the side of too weak a solution, because too strong a one can cause the death of the root ends and eventually of the plant.

Fertilizers can be made from organic substances such as seaweed (which is rich in trace elements), or from inorganic chemicals. Both have the same effect if properly used. Some fertilizers have more nitrogen than others and it is those rich in nitrogen which give the plant a deep green colour and are good for making leaves. But if you have a plant which is grown for its flowers or berries you are more likely to obtain a good show if you use a fertilizer rich in potash, such as one made for tomatoes.

Never give fertilizer, even in liquid form, to a dry plant, but only when the soil is moist, and do not give more feeds than the plant can use or you will get a concentration of unwanted fertilizer in the soil which could kill the plant. Once in 10 or 14 days is ample even for fast–growing plants. It is a mistake to think that because the plant is growing slowly that it needs more fertilizer. If growth has not speeded up after one dose look to see what else could be slowing it up.

Plants need a higher temperature in which to grow than in which to exist. Poor light, too little or too much water, any damage to the roots caused by drowning, by pest attack or by tearing, such as when a plant roots through its pot and the roots are broken when the pot is moved, can all make growth impossible.

Some house plants can be fed with foliar feed, that is weak fertilizer solutions sprayed on to the leaves, but this does not suit some of the shiny–leaved varieties, the leaves of which mark badly.

Containers

Pot plants, other than bulbs which are not going to stay long in their containers, should be grown in well–drained pots, not bowls—which waterlog too easily. Plastic ones are lighter and easier to keep clean, but clay pots lose more water to the air and thus create a more humid atmosphere.

Pots need some sort of base or container to protect the furniture on which they are to stand. It may be a simple plant saucer or an elaborate bowl, either of which will collect the drainage water. Unless housing large specimens a collection of odd pots and bowls makes a room look rather untidy; the best way to overcome this is to group the plants together, using the various colours, shapes and textures as one would when arranging flowers. A big plant on the floor can have smaller ones grouped around its base. A trough which will house several pots, especially those which need the humidity that can be supplied by packing them round with damp peat, is also fine for housing trailers, and is best on a stand fitted with castors so that the whole group can be moved together.

Another method of grouping plants is on a plant pole. This is a spring–loaded pole placed between floor and ceiling joist which has plant pot holders in pairs at different levels all the way up the pole. As the pot holders can be fixed at different spacings to suit the plants they are fine for tall plants and trailers. Each holder takes a pot with its saucer balanced by a similarly weighted one on the other side. The next pair should be set at right angles to the first and in this way a whole column of plants can be housed easily. The pole can be situated near a tall window or in a corner of a room if supplied with extra light and the lighting strip can be placed upright to accentuate the height. As the fixtures and the whole pole can be swung round if care is used it is possible to vary the effect and to give plants a change of light intensity.

Pots can also be grouped on water trays, in which case they will not need saucers or be hidden by bowls.

At festive seasons florists have a habit of making up mixed bowls of pot plants, lovely to look at for that particular moment of time, but unfortunately not usually requiring the same treatment or growing at the same rate. If the plants are still in their tiny pots these can be extracted and a fresh assortment made, but unfortunately some will be growing in the soil and then the highest minimum temperature requirement will have to be used for the whole group, at least until you can dismantle the lot. Those in very small pots will need to be repotted, if they are true house plants which you are planning to keep.

Repotting

Repotting can be of two kinds: to a larger pot, in which case the excess space below and around (but not above) the present pot ball is filled with new soil mix, or again in the same sized pot, when some of the old soil mixture should be carefully removed and replaced by fresh. The first is used for all actively growing plants, the second for plants in their resting period just before new growth is expected.

The soil in the pot to be treated must be moistened and the plant then carefully tapped out. If it has an obvious stem put the fingers of one hand on both sides of this to hold the plant and soil as it is inverted, and tap the pot against any hard surface, such as the edge of a kitchen unit, to loosen the soil ball from the sides of the pot. Usually, however, house plants tend to be bushy and to flop all over the edge of the pot. This means that to loosen the soil by tapping the top edge is well nigh impossible. Grip the plant by its base as far as is possible, then tap all round the sides of the pot, when the soil ball will gradually loosen, and the pot can be drawn off sideways.

Peat mixtures need no firming, only tapping to settle the fresh mix into place. Loam mixtures are firmed round the edge with the fingers.

Insect pests which cannot be controlled by washing or brushing off can be sprayed with an insecticide such as resmethrin

Handling for Health

By handling your plants regularly, removing any dead leaves or flowers, you soon get to know if your treatment is right. Be on the look out for pests, which are not usually a hazard indoors, but it will save a lot of time and worry if these are killed as soon as seen. The most likely ones to occur are aphids (greenflies and their allies) which attack the soft growing tips of plants and the undersides of leaves. If only a few are there they can be brushed off into a bowl of soapy water with a fine paint brush rather than the oft–recommended method of squashing them with your fingers, for this is no good for young growth. The other pest under leaves is the red spider mite, but you can only see this with the aid of a hand lens, though occasionally some web is present. They cause leaves to look greyish and mottled, and occur only if the air is insufficiently humid. The plant should be sprayed or washed with clear water or with an insecticide (except in such cases as are mentioned). White oil emulsion or resmethrin are the safest.

Whiteflies are sometimes brought into the house on plants from a friend's greenhouse, and will prob-ably have been transported in the im-mature, immobile form of the pest on the underside of the leaves. The whitefly itself, in the adult stage, flies off the plant at the least movement. This makes it tricky to spray. The best method is to isolate it as soon as the flies are seen, by enveloping it in a large polythene bag, dropped with great care over the top of it. Then spray resmethrin in through a gap in the bottom. You will have to keep it covered for a fortnight and spray every second or third day, because the spray only kills the adult whiteflies and not the eggs or larval stages.

Occasionally you will find you have imported a scale insect or two on a plant (they will not have flown in at the window or been brought in on a bunch of garden flowers). They look like little greyish blobs and are usually on the stem or under the leaves near the veins and they do not move when you touch the plant. They can be picked off, or killed by touching with a spot of methylated spirit on the end of a matchstick or paint brush.

If you should be so unlucky as to import vine weevil grubs in the soil of the pot they will probably have eaten through the collar of the plant just below ground level before you realize you have them. This sometimes occurs with primulas. Just cut your losses and dispose of both plant and soil without spreading the pest.

The most likely disease is grey mould or botrytis, which can become a nuisance at temperatures below 10°C (50°F) in dull weather. Increasing the temperature always helps. Diseased parts of the plant must be carefully removed.

Cleaning house plants
Some leaves will die of old age and have to be removed. Always do this right up to the end of the leaf stalk or the dead piece may cause disease to spread to the stem. Other leaves will need to be washed to remove dust and, in some areas, industrial grime. If clear water does not remove the dirt a small amount of detergent can be used, well mixed in the sponging water, but some plants will not tolerate any additive. Specially prepared additives are sold for washing large leaves, but if these are found to leave a varnish–like deposit on the leaves they should not be used as they will have a deleterious effect in the long run. If leaves are infested with red spider mites the correct dose of insecticide can be added to the washing water in place of detergent. Always finish with a clear water rinse and

make sure water is not lodged between leaf and stem or in the folds of leaves, for these are the places where rot often starts.

Small–leaved plants can be dipped head first into water if the soil is held in with a cloth or polythene. Do not wave the plants about and drain them carefully before upending them again. Ferns with finely cut leaves should only be misted, not even sprayed.

Holiday Care

Short absences
These are not difficult to cope with provided the plants are on a water tray or in self–watering pots. If neither is available water before departing and move the plants out of direct sunshine. If the weather is cold it is essential to keep the temperature at least at the mimimum. This may mean putting all the plants in one room. If it is impossible to maintain even the minimum required temperature do *not* water before leaving home. Plants will withstand cold better if on the dry side.

Longer absences
If somebody is willing to water even once a week put all plants with similar requirements together and as near the

Remove dust and industrial grime from glossy-leaved plants by sponging the leaves with either water or a weak detergent solution

Plants can be grouped on a tray of moist gravel if they have to be left for a few days without attention

source of water as possible. A list of instructions may or may not prove a help! Do not ask for feeding, cleaning or other services.

If automatic watering trays are in use make sure the water will last out the absence by installing a larger bottle. Individual plants can be raised above their waterfilled saucers by blocks of wood, provided a wick can be inserted to suck up the water (as in a clay pot on a tray).

The easiest method of all is to swathe each large plant in polythene and put a polythene bag over each smaller one and then put the pots close together in a shady place. They will last out 10 to 14 days like this with little harm. Anything you value greatly or needing temperatures much above those outside is best parked out with another house plant enthusiast or even with your regular nurseryman.

Permanent residents

Considered in this section are plants which can be grown for long periods in the home, though some do need the added protection of a bottle, dome or indoor plant cabinet.

They are almost all grown for the beauty of their evergreen foliage, which is frequently variegated, and this, with the many contrasts in habit, allows the possibility of making groupings as pleasing as those of any flower arranger. Although many of these plants will produce flowers in the house, those which are more completely dependent on flowers for their charm have a very long season in bloom. The few plants included which are deciduous (that is, lose all their leaves at one season) are ones which can withstand being put in some inconspicuous place, even a cool airy cupboard, for a short period.

Adiantum

These are the maidenhair ferns, the two commonest being *Adiantum capillus–veneris* which is almost hardy, and *A. cuneatum*, which needs a minimum temperature of 10°C (50°F) or it will lose its leaves. These are best grown in a Wardian case or plastic dome when small, as their thin, very finely divided fronds need high humidity and suffer badly in air polluted by tobacco smoke or fumes. If kept with other house plants move them well away before spraying the rest with insecticide and do not return them until all vapour has gone. Keep well watered in a soil mix rich in peat or leafmould.

Aechmea fasciata

Aechmeas are members of the bromeliad family which produce their thick strap–shaped leaves on such a short stem that they form a container or 'vase' in the centre. In nature this collects rainwater and it is through this that you should water the plants. *Aechmea fasciata*, the most likely species to be available, has leaves barred with silver and a flower spike of pink bracts with blue flowers. To obtain other species it may be necessary to contact a specialist. All have very highly coloured bracts, flowers and berries, giving long–lasting colour. After producing berries the whole vase dies, leaving off–shoots to carry on. Some are difficult to get to flower indoors and there are commercial nurseries which treat them with chemicals to assist the process.

Keep in a good light or give artificial light when natural light is bad. Aechmeas will stand wide temperature variations, with a minimum winter temperature of 7°C (45°F). They are easily grown in pots of peat mix, but they can be unpotted and have their roots wrapped in sphagnum moss and secured between pieces of bark (use plastic covered wire), for in nature many are found lodged in the branches of tropical trees.

Aichryson domesticum variegatum

Also known as *Aeonium domesticum variegatum*, this is a small plant from the Canary Islands with cream–variegated succulent leaves on trailing shoots. The yellow sedum–like flowers are best removed. It will stand minimum temperatures of 7°C (45°F), but grows better at 13°C (55°F). It needs a light position but does well without direct sunlight. It is easily overwatered.

Aloe

Aloes make good house plants only if given good light, either natural or augmented. Then, of the smaller ones, *Aloe variegata*, the partridge aloe, develops its fine grey and white markings; the leaves of *A. plicata* make a fine fan of blue–grey colour, and *A. striata* develops its coral edge. These three come from South Africa. They need well–drained, gritty soil, a moderate amount of water given from below, and a minimum winter temperature of 10°C (50°F). Their flowers are in loose spikes and usually brick red.

Ananas

These are the pineapples (bromeliads), the variegated forms of which are worth growing as foliage plants. There are two kinds, *Ananas comosus variegatus* (also known as *A. sativus variegatus*) which has rather broad, cream–edged grey–green leaves, often with a pink flush, and *A. bracteatus*

striatus, with yellow–edged green leaves which reach one full metre (3ft). As all leaves are saw–edged the plants need placing on a stand where they can curve out without interference, for if caught on flesh or on material they may be bent, and once bent the leaf never recovers. The young leaves spot easily if water rests on them so it is usually easiest to water from below, either by using a permanent wick from the drainage hole into a reservoir or by filling the saucer in which the pot is standing. In this case excess must not be given, for if the roots in the base of the pot become waterlogged the tips of the leaves may die.

The pineapples can be acclimatized down to 10°C (50°F), but do best at 18°C (65°F) or over. They can withstand quite dry air conditions. The small fruits occasionally formed are not really edible; for this a commercial variety is needed which has larger, more succulent fruits.

Top
Adiantum capillus-veneris

Bottom
Aichryson domesticum variegatum

Left
Left to right: *Citrus mitis, Hedera helix* Glacier and *Ficus benjamina*

Araucaria excelsa

Although not often offered as a house plant *Araucaria araucana*, the monkey puzzle tree, which can sometimes be bought young from a tree nursery, also makes an interesting pot plant. Its young leaves are bright green and the stems droop.

All will exist away from windows, but should be given a fair amount of light when growing in spring and summer, and need turning regularly to prevent them becoming one sided. Water well and feed occasionally during growth, but do not overfeed or the plant will try to make more growth than it has light for. They exist at 7°C (45°F) and put up with tobacco smoke and fumes.

Asparagus spp.
The so-called asparagus ferns are not true ferns but related to the vegetable asparagus. In their unselected forms they are climbers (or trailers), but more generally useful as pot plants are *Asparagus plumosus nanus*, *A. p. compactus* and *A. sprengeri compactus*, all of which are dwarf. *A. plumosus* varieties have tiny needle-like leaves, ½cm (¼in) long; those of *A. sprengeri* are long, 2cm (1in), and narrow. If your dwarf plant suddenly sends up a climbing shoot you can either train it on a light frame or cut it out at the base. The stems are very wiry and often develop small spines.

Asparagus asparagoides, called smilax, is also occasionally used as a house plant. It differs in having very shiny, roughly oval leaves and is a much-branched plant, climbing by its many spines.

All will put up with shady positions and low (though not freezing) temperatures. Keep watered regularly when in growth or they will drop their leaves. Feed occasionally and cut out old stems carefully in spring to make way for new growths. Pot on as necessary, using a fast-draining mix.

Aspidistra elatior
The Victorian favourite *Aspidistra elatior* and its scarce form *A. e. variegata*, with pale cream stripes, are now returning to favour. They have fine shining leaves growing from a basal rhizome, and will put up with low temperatures, 7°C (45°F), rather poor light, any soil and erratic watering, though obviously paying for better care. They grow slowly but when it can be seen clearly that the root stock has branched they can easily be divided to make two plants. Do not wash the leaves with anything but clear water.

Aphelandra squarrosa louisae
This is a very striking Brazilian shrub which as a pot plant is renewed every second year, so it never takes up much room. The leaves grow in pairs and are a glossy deep green with the veins picked out in white; it is sometimes called the zebra plant. It reacts badly to erratic watering and is best grown on a wet sand tray or plastic matting in a light place out of direct sunshine, with an optimum winter temperature of 16 to 18°C (60 to 65°F), which should never fall below 13°C (55°F).

You will probably have acquired this plant in autumn when it normally bears its bright, deep yellow spikes or bracts enclosing inconspicuous pale yellow flowers, and if you get one just coming into flower these bracts will give colour for three months. Nearer Christmas, unless the grower has kept it back by night length control, its flower life will be much less. After

flowering, cut off the spikes and do not feed until the new shoots break out. Then repot and feed fortnightly.

These plants become straggly if grown on for too many years and do not produce such good spikes. There are some varieties of *Aphelandra squarrosa* which are grown for their leaves alone, with more closely packed growth or whiter markings.

For growth use a good general liquid fertilizer, but for flowering a high potash tomato fertilizer will give better results, and such plants should be kept in the smallest pots that will contain the roots.

Araucaria spp.
Araucaria excelsa (or *heterophylla*) the Norfolk Island pine, was one of the trees used as a house plant by the Victorians, who could only manage really tough plants. Nurserymen propagate from both *Araucaria excelsa* and *A. columnaris* (which looks very similar when young) and these normally make a fine straight stem and whorls of flat branches. Occasionally a side growth is rooted instead of tip growth and the resultant plant decides to lie outwards and if not firmly staked will make a bush.

Right
Aphelandra squarrosa louisae

Asparagus plumosus nanus

Asplenium *spp.*

Two species of asplenium are used as house plants. *Asplenium bulbiferum*, known as the mother spleenwort, has large, finely divided fronds from which tiny plantlets are produced on the upper surface. In contrast the other, *A. nidus*, has fine undivided fronds, rather like the British native hart's tongue fern, but larger. Both need high humidity, such as can be given easily in a tall Wardian case, or when young in a dome. They can be kept moist if the pot is surrounded by damp peat, but this must not prevent the free drainage of the pot which should contain peat mix and grit. They can be misted over with clear water, but should not be sprayed with a forceful jet of water, nor washed over with anything but clear water, as they damage very easily. They do well in bathrooms if a minimum temperature of 13°C (55°F) can be maintained for *A. nidus*, 10°C (50°F) for *A. bulbiferum*.

Begonia *spp. and hybrids*

Better than any of the flowering forms of begonia for use as house plants are the *Begonia rex* hybrids, which are grown solely for their finely coloured patterned leaves, and *Begonia masoniana*, which is rather similar in leaf texture, but has much smaller green leaves marked with an almost black 'iron cross'.

These begonias can be grown in very shady places, though the colours are improved with good diffused light. They are difficult to keep growing at temperatures less than 13°C (55°F), and as they grow most in the winter this should be regarded as barely sufficient, for there will be little sun heat at this season. They also need high humidity to do well. Spray the air around them rather than the leaf surface which is highly crinkled in most forms and liable to hold the water. The leaves last for very long periods, but if in too dry an atmosphere or if the plant becomes water-logged they die round the edges.

If the temperature drops too low or the air around the plant becomes stagnant in your effort to keep it humid *Begonia rex* leaves may become mildewed. Keep them warmer and dust with flowers of sulphur or a good fungicide such as benomyl before the mildew spreads to other leaves and the crown of the plant.

Begonia rex extends its rhizome out sideways, which means it needs a relatively wide pot. A half pot usually does very well. Never let the plant be short of room and give it an occasional feed of a liquid fertilizer with a high nitrogen content.

Beloperone guttata

The shrimp plant is a small shrub, 61cm (2ft), grown for its attractive shrimp–pink bracts—lime green in one variety—rather than for any beauty of its small white flowers, or for its arching habit. You would hardly look twice at its leaves. Fortunately it flowers almost throughout the year provided a temperature of 13°C (55°F) can be guaranteed as a minimum: below that it loses its leaves and hibernates. Never let the temperature fall below 7°C (45°F). Keep in good diffused light and water moderately during the summer, very little in winter. The plant can be pruned back in early spring to make it branch out again, and this is essential if it has lost its leaves or become leggy. This is a plant which pays for feeding regularly with tomato fertilizer, especially when it is producing shrimp after shrimp. Be sure to repot whenever necessary as if pot bound it will over flower and lose its quality.

There is a dwarf form which only reaches 30cm (1ft), but it is rarely available.

Billbergia *spp.*

Billbergias are bromeliads which do not usually make quite such fine 'vases' as aechmeas do, but which produce amusingly coloured spikes, for example with pink bracts and red flowers tipped with blue, though they are not so long lasting as those of many bromeliads. Their narrow leaves are also less effective. They produce lots of offsets which makes them easier to buy in flower and keep going, than is the case with aechmea.

The commonest is *Billbergia nutans*, with pink bracts and green and blue flowers, but there are many others, and I recommend selecting them by sight. *B. windii*, if obtainable, is an improvement on *B. nutans* as its leaves are wider.

They are best grown in pots of peat mix in a minimum temperature of 10°C (50°F) and well watered from above during the summer.

Very dilute liquid fertilizer or foliar feed can be sprayed on to the leaves if this is easier than trying to find the soil in the pot—the leaves of *B. nutans* are apt to flop over the edge.

Asparagus sprengeri

Calathea makoyana

This genus would be difficult to include among easy house plants were it not for the plastic domes which will provide the foolproof humid growing atmosphere required here. Your job is then to keep the dome, in which the peat mix may be wetter than usual but with plenty of charcoal in the base, in a room where the temperature will not fall below 18°C (65°F).

Calathea makoyana, the peacock plant, is the least difficult of the calatheas and should have a dome of its own. It has most fascinating patterns of pale and dark green on top and a wonderful purplish red back. All calatheas have this red back and many have beautiful feather markings on top. It is not easy to distinguish them from marantas, under which name many are sold. Curiously the colours are better in shade than in sun, and they should all be kept in the shade. *Calathea makoyana* hates smoke and fumes and the quickest way to kill it is to use an aerosol spray anywhere near it.

Chlorophytum comosum variegatum

This spider plant is one of the easiest of house plants. It has long cream-striped leaves in a rosette from which come arching stems bearing miniature plants which may go on to bear still more plantlets in their turn. Any of these plantlets can be rooted by pegging them down into a little pot of compost.

It looks fine hanging on a plant pole or wall bracket and a big enough plant merits a palm stand.

Provided it is not actually frozen it will survive low temperatures, and will grow in quite shady places, but these conditions do not produce the best results. The chlorophytum needs watering freely when actively growing in spring and summer, less in winter. If kept in very poor light the leaves become thin and the stripes are less obvious, and if dried out the leaf margins go brown.

Cissus spp.

The kangaroo vine, *Cissus antarctica*, climbs vigorously by means of tendrils. Its fresh green leaves have red stalks. It is normally evergreen, but if in too warm and dry an atmosphere the leaves turn brown and eventually drop off. It will put up with poor light and cool conditions (7 to 10°C, 45 to 50°F) if the air is sufficiently humid. Do not feed it often if you do not wish to be taken over. If you cannot provide a sufficiently large frame for it to climb it can be reduced to a column or a bush by judicious pinching out of all stem ends, and by doing this regularly for a few years you can obtain a trunk like a vine, which you

will no longer have to stake, covered with twiggy growths smothered with leaves.

Cissus discolor, from Java, is more exacting, but worth the extra heat and humidity it needs to produce its large green leaves, silvered between the veins and purple below. It is not reliably evergreen and may lose its leaves at any time (especially in the winter) as the result of too low a temperature and badly drained soil.

Cissus striata, from South America, has deeper green leaves each of five small leaflets, and makes a smaller climbing or trailing plant. It is not so tolerant of bad conditions as *C. antarctica*.

Citrus spp.

If you just want fine green foliage it is easy to raise this from pips of citrus fruits, but if you would like the sweet–smelling flowers of orange blossom in spring and summer followed by brilliant edible little fruits you should get *Citrus mitis*, the calamondin orange, as this will flower when still tiny provided it has enough light in summer to ripen the stems. If you have a sunny window or balcony you should achieve good results; if not, additional lighting may make fruiting possible, but *C. mitis* needs a higher minimum winter temperature (13°C, 55°F) than those species grown from pips for their foliage alone. Never let the plant get dry in summer or overwater in winter. Feed with liquid fertilizer every 14 days from spring to autumn, and pot on as necessary, using JIP.3.

Codiaeum variegatum

Codiaeums are more frequently known as crotons. They have shiny, thick, excitingly multi-coloured leaves which vary in shape between plain oval or lance shaped and deeply lobed, smooth or fluted. Most of the leaves have a base colour of yellow, overlaid with green, red or bronze and almost any mixture can occur on the same plant.

They need bright sunlight or additional lighting to keep the colours brilliant, and the constant temperature of thermostatically controlled central heating with a minimum of 16°C (60°F). They drop their lower leaves if chilled. For this reason, too, cold tap water should be avoided; use water at room temperature and spray occasionally with clear water or with resmethrin if any soft scale insects or red spider mites have appeared. Do not cut out any unwanted shoots when the plant is in full growth as the stem will pump out unbelievable quantities of white latex—it is of the euphorbia family. If any pruning has to be done choose the winter when

Aspidistra elatior variegata

Opposite
Asplenium bulbiferum

A wide variation in leaf colouring is shown in these three varieties of *Begonia rex*

Right
Begonia masoniana

Right
Calathea makoyana

Opposite, right
Fatshedera lizei (left) and *Platycerium*
bifurcatum (right)

Cissus antarctica

growth is at its slowest and be ready to apply finely powdered charcoal or vine styptic to the wound to check the bleeding.

Cordyline terminalis

This is often called dracaena and is surely the species to which the name dragon plant belongs. It has long leaves, usually variegated with red and occasionally with a white stripe. The young leaves of good strains are almost pure red. It enjoys the same conditions as dracaenas (see page 39), and will eventually form a tall, stalked specimen if the conditions suit it. At all times it should be placed where the crown can be clearly seen.

Cryptanthus spp.

These are very small members of the bromeliad family, with spiny–edged, very finely striped or mottled leaves which are spread out at ground level, giving them the common names of earth stars and starfish. *Cryptanthus acaulis*, its variety *ruber*, and *C. bivittatus* are indispensable for bottle gardens, where they revel in the high humidity. *C. zonatus* looks better outside where the cross marking of the leaves is more readily appreciated. Try it carefully packed around the base with sphagnum, wired to a cork–encrusted log. The leaf colours (greens, creams, pinks and browns), are improved by good light. If growing it in a pot ensure good humidity by placing it on wet pebbles. Water

can also be given from above but these plants do not have the vase of aechmea to hold water. Use peat mix, and keep a minimum winter temperature of 13°C (55°F).

Cussonia spicata

Cussonia is closely allied to schefflera (see page 66), but its sub–divided or wavy leaflets give it a lighter appearance. It needs careful staking as its stems are very brittle, and should be repotted in JIP.3 as necessary, for it grows very rapidly and will not tolerate being pot bound, losing its lower leaves. Discard when too big.

Cyperus alternifolius

This is a sedge allied to papyrus, which is often called the umbrella grass because the narrow leaves are in a whorl at the top of the stem (like the ribs of an umbrella) where the insignificant flowers and more interesting 'seeds' are grouped. It makes a pleasant contrast to most other foliage plants, and can be grown in loamy soil in a well–watered pot or in a deep bowl in which the water may cover the soil. This is the plant for a small indoor pool as it will live in up to 15cm (6in) of water. The type plant can reach 1m (3ft), but there is a slightly less vigorous variegated form, and a very effective variety known as *gracilis* which is about 38 to 45cm (15 to 18in) high, a pleasing deep green and with stiffer leaves than the type, which can

become rather shaggy looking after a while.

Cyperus really need a minimum winter temperature of 13°C (55°F), and if there is any likelihood of this also being the maximum it is best to keep the soil on the dry side. If dried out they go yellowish brown and you will have to wait for fresh growth.

Cyrtomium falcatum

Commonly known as the holly fern, this plant has fine shiny fronds with segments roughly the shape of the common holly leaf. It is one of the easier house plants as it will not only put up with poor light, but actually needs shade in sunny weather. It will survive in temperatures down to 7°C (45°F) in winter. Although it will live in relatively dry conditions it is wise to remember that it is a fern and water regularly and spray occasionally. Do not let it become pot bound but move it on to the next sized pot in the spring when the young fronds are just appearing.

Dieffenbachia arvida exotica

Dieffenbachias are tropical members of the arum family, but grown for their leaves which are large and usually profusely marked with ivory or cream. The easiest to obtain and most likely to do well is *Dieffenbachia arvida exotica*. This really needs a temperature of 18°C (65°F), but can be gradually acclimatized to slightly less; a fairly good light produces the best colour, and a humid atmosphere is essential. Dieffenbachias are best grown in thermostatically controlled centrally heated rooms out of direct sunlight, and surrounded by moist peat or stood on wet pebbles. They need a rich soil mix (JIP.3) and should be regularly watered and sprayed. If you have to leave them for more than a day or two leave on the central heating, put a wick from the base of the pot into a water reservoir and surround the plants with plastic film.

The sap is poisonous and contact with it should be avoided.

Dizygotheca elegantissima

It is the juvenile leaf form of this Australian shrub (often known as *Aralia elegantissima*) which makes an interesting foliage plant, having very palmately divided leaves which have roughly the same effect as those of cyperus, but with the umbrellas being more widely spaced on the plant. The leaves start a coppery–red colour but soon turn deep green.

This plant needs a good light position out of direct sun in a thermostatically controlled warm room (18°C, 65°F minimum) and should be well watered, but must be in a fast–draining soil. If the temperature drops too low or the plant becomes waterlogged the leaves will fall.

Its leaves are liable to attack by red spider mite in too dry an atmosphere so spray regularly, for the leaves are fussy to sponge. If red spider mite does appear, spraying with resmethrin will kill it.

Red– and green–variegated varieties of *Codiaeum variegatum*

Opposite
Chlorophytum comosum variegatum

Dracaena spp.

Dracaenas (which are frequently confused with cordylines) include many high–temperature, high–humidity species, but there are three which can make satisfactory house plants given a minimum winter temperature of 13°C (55°F). All are grown for their variegated evergreen leaves. The roughly oval ones of *Dracaena godseffiana* are green spotted with white and there is a variant with cream. *D. sanderiana* has longer, narrower leaves edged with ivory; and those of *D. marginata concinna* (which may be in rather short supply) are almost grass–like, striped with cream and margined with red. Like all variegated leaves they are at their best given good but diffused light. *D. sanderiana* can grow to 1 or 1·25m (3 or 4ft) before beginning to lose any basal leaves provided it is carefully fed and watered, and given a centrally heated room kept at 16°C (60°F). Both *D. fragrans massangeana* and *D. f. lindenii* will grow slowly to 1·5 or 2m (5 or 6ft). The first has cream central stripes to its leaves and the second has cream margins.

Spray occasionally to keep the air moist, but do not let the water remain in the leaf bases. A rich potting compost (JIP.3) is needed for these plants, and they appreciate being planted out into indoor beds or shallow tubs where they can extend their roots.

Fatshedera lizei

This hybrid between *Fatsia japonica* and the ivy, *Hedera helix*, is a most useful pot plant in fairly cool rooms. It has rather large, bright green leaves, divided like ivy, and there is another form with cream edges to the leaves. Its rather sprawling habit enables it to be trained on a trellis to make a wall cover or a screen, or it can be allowed to trail from the pot on to the floor. It sprawls most in poor light. This plant will survive temperatures of 4 to 7°C (40 to 45°F), and prefers to be cool rather than too warm. When in active growth feed with liquid fertilizer to obtain the biggest leaves, which need to be kept washed. Spray with resmethrin if red spider mite appears.

Fatsia japonica

This plant, occasionally called *Aralia sieboldii*, is a definite bush with more deeply incised leaves than those of its offspring, the fatshedera. It is hardy enough to be grown outdoors in mild places, so does well in cool rooms such as halls, where it can be put in shady places. There is a rather scarce form edged irregularly with cream. This does not do so well as the green form which makes a fine specimen bush if kept watered well in summer, and fed about once a month from spring to late summer. Wash the leaves as necessary.

Top
Dizygotheca elegantissima

Left
Cordyline terminalis

Opposite
Cyperus alternifolius gracilis

Ficus spp.

This genus of figs contains house plants as different as the large and tough rubber plant, *Ficus elastica*, the daintily pendulous *F. benjamina*, and the slender small–leaved climbers, *F. pumila* and *F. radicans*, both of which make aerial roots. *Ficus elastica*, usually grown in its improved form *robusta*, has large, tough, shiny green, leaves; it can grow into a fine specimen in spacious, warm places which can be kept at a temperature between 10 and 16°C (50 and 60°F). Unless the terminal bud (which has a handsome pink sheath) is removed the rubber plant does not branch, but will keep its leaves right down to the ground for many years provided it has been kept warm and not overwatered. If the bottom leaves have fallen or the top has reached as far as you want it to go, prune off the top in late winter and the stem will throw out side shoots. Water sparingly in winter, especially if the temperature is lower than it should be, but copiously when the plant is growing fast. It is important to keep the leaves clean; water is best for this. It stands shade well.

There are also variegated forms of the type which need better lighting for their best colour, and a purple–leaved one called Black Prince is the most recent introduction.

Ficus benjamina, which has quite small leaves, 5cm (2in), is apt to take up rather a lot of room since it branches freely and its branches are pendulous, but it makes a pleasant feature for three or four years. It needs higher temperatures than *F. e. robusta*, about 16 to 21°C (60 to 70°F).

The creeper *F. pumila* is almost hardy (minimum 7°C, 45°F), branches well and can be used as a trailer on plant stands or wall brackets. It has a cream–variegated form, but the creeping fig often used to light up a bottle garden is *F. radicans variegata*. You must be prepared to prune it occasionally. This needs a minimum temperature of 13 to 16°C (55 to 60°F). All this group will climb up a plastic wire column filled with sphagnum moss to make a living pillar. If the moss is kept constantly moist they will not suffer from attack by red spider mite.

Fittonia vershaffeltii

This is an herbaceous creeper with soft, deep green leaves veined in carmine in the type, in rose in variety *pearcei* and in cream in *argyroneura*. It is most chancy in an open room, disliking draughts and fumes, and needing a minimum temperature of 16°C (60°F), but if kept in a plastic dome, with soil on the dry side and well drained below, so that it has humid air but no waterlogging, it will root into any soil its shoots can reach. Because of this habit it occasionally becomes necessary to prune it in a dome or it swamps other slower growing occupants. In a bottle it is worthy of being grown alone for even though growing more slowly there than anywhere else, it can spread. Never take a fittonia anywhere where an aerosol has been used. It is incredibly sensitive to air pollution.

I have recently bought a much more reliable fittonia for use in rooms, known as *F. argyroneura nana*, which has smaller, cream–veined leaves. It is making pleasant ground cover for a mixed planting.

Bottom left
Dracaena fragrans lindenii

Bottom right
Dracaena fragrans massangeana

Opposite
Dracaena marginata concinna

Top row, left to right: *Hedera helix* Green Ripple, *H. helix* Glacier, *Dieffenbachia arvida exotica*. Bottom row, left to right: *Peperomia magnoliaefolia*, Saintpaulias, pink and blue, *Beloperone guttata* and *Hedera helix lutzii*

Right
Plastic tower pots. Top, left to right: *Gynura sarmentosa*, *Neanthe bella*, *Saintpaulia ionantha* and *Scindapsus aureus*. Bottom, left to right: *Scindapsus aureus* and *Chlorophytum comosum variegatum*

Gardenia jasminoides

Gardenias are grown as small ever-green shrubs for their richly scented, double, white flowers, which are produced mainly in summer, but with a few at other seasons. They are definitely shrubs for a warmer thermostatically controlled room, needing a minimum temperature of 13°C (55°F) to exist, 18°C (65°F) to do any good in winter, and even more in summer. They are very clearly acid soil plants, which need distilled or boiled and cooled water for both watering and spraying. If the leaves show signs of losing their deep green colour do not wait until they have gone yellow but apply iron sequestrol according to the maker's instructions. A very dilute solution of Epsom salts will sometimes also improve the leaf colour.

Use a peat soil mix containing a little flowers of sulphur and enough grit to make drainage very free, for if waterlogged gardenias drop their flower buds almost at once and their leaves in a steady succession. Feed occasionally during the summer with a liquid fertilizer such as a seaweed extract.

Grevillea robusta

This silk oak is an Australian tree, but it is easily raised from seed and makes a good house plant for two or three years. The leaves are very large but finely dissected like some ferns, giving a light feathery effect. It needs bright light and regular turning round to keep it growing straight, and its roots are sensitive to over– and under–watering, both causing the lower, normally evergreen leaves to turn yellow and fall, which spoils it as a specimen plant. Because of its need for good light it is not easy to hide the bare stem behind a bank of other plants. The young leaves are often bronzed with fine hairs.

Grevillea robusta can be overwintered in a temperature as low as 7°C (45°F) and is best grown cool at all times. Feed with liquid fertilizer at 14–day intervals during its period of rapid growth in spring and summer, to ensure really large leaves.

Left
Fatsia japonica

Top
Grevillea robusta

45

Top
Ficus elastica Black Prince

Bottom
Ficus elastica tricolor

Right
Ficus radicans variegata

Opposite
A short-term arrangement of house plants in a plastic planter. The ivy is *Hedera canariensis variegata*

Gynura sarmentosa

This is the most readily available species in Britain. *Gynura aurantiaca* does not differ greatly from it except that it is more upright in habit, *G. sarmentosa* being a trailer. It has deep green leaves with a thick velvety covering of violet hairs, which need a good light to develop their full colour. The plant grows rapidly if fed and watered regularly in a peat compost in a minimum temperature of 16°C (60°F). It pays for frequent pinching, both to keep the shoots branching and manageable and also to delay the time of flowering. The flowers are sparse, weedy looking and of a most brilliant orange. Replace after two years, by which time the plant has usually become rather difficult to keep bushy.

Hedera spp.

These are the ivies, aerial rooting, evergreen climbers, of which there are very many distinct varieties, some of the hardy common ivy which will grow in any cool situation, and of the slightly tender Canary Island ivy which is usually grown in its cream–variegated form, *Hedera canariensis variegata*. This grows best in a temperature of 10°C (50°F) or more. All these ivies will grow in shade, but the colours of the variegated forms are always much more distinct in bright, diffused light.

Ivies do not like hot, dry rooms and lose their fresh green colour if the air is too dry. They are also liable then to become infested with red spider mite, which can be killed by spraying with resmethrin. Keep well watered, pot on in JIP.2 or peat compost, feed moderately throughout spring and summer, and brush out any dead leaves when cleaning the plants.

Ivy leaves come in many variations of the typical five–lobed leaf; for example, in *sagittaefolia* the lobes are very narrow, in Green Ripple they are waved, and in several others deep green, very small and crowded. It is easier to pick what you want than to describe them. The variegated ones range from Gold Heart, with yellow–centred leaves which prefers to grow upwards and does not branch readily; Glacier where the cream overlaps the green, making it look grey, and which is much used in mixed containers; Little Diamond which takes kindly to being grafted on top of fatshedera stems to make little standards (do not let the stem grow any side shoots); to the one for big displays, the variegated Canary Island ivy, which can be trained up screens, make a column or be draped along container edges. There is also a yellow–speckled one, *marmorata*, which always makes me think it has red spider mite, even before this is true.

Heptapleurum arboricola

This is really a schefflera (see page 66), though always sold as heptapleurum. It is smaller leaved and daintier than *Schefflera actinophylla*, and is best treated like *S. digitata* and made into a bush. It will stand a minimum winter temperature of 10°C (50°F), but needs 16°C (60°F) for growth.

Fittonia vershaffeltii argyroneura

Hibiscus rosa-sinensis

This hibiscus is a fine shrub with large, mallow–like flowers often 12 to 15cm (5 to 6in) across and usually red, pink or yellow, which are produced in summer. The flowers usually last only one day, but a good specimen is rarely out of flower as a bud is made in most leaf axils. The leaves are interesting in shape.

It needs a warm, sunny room with a minimum temperature of 13°C (55°F) if it is to be kept evergreen throughout the year. Watering must be frequent throughout the summer or the plant will stop producing flowers. Pot on if absolutely necessary in JIP.3, but keep it in as small a pot as possible as the plant then makes flowers rather than very large leaves. Prune out or shorten any badly misplaced shoots, and keep a look out for greenflies.

If during the winter the temperature drops below 13°C (55°F) the leaves will go yellow and drop, and the plant will need little water at that time. It can be hard pruned in early spring to encourage it to make strong new growth in a temperature of 18°C (65°F), when a good bush can be remade. It requires very good light at this stage and pays for some temporary additional lighting.

Howea spp.

There are two plants of this name, both liable to be called kentia. The commonest and hardiest is *Howea fosteriana*, an old favourite of the Victorians and the one referred to always as a potted palm, which does well in moderately light rooms with a minimum temperature of 10°C (50°F). The other, *H. belmoreana*, is not so strong growing and has smaller leaves, but needs a temperature of 16°C (60°F) in winter. Both need little water in winter, but more while growing during the spring and summer, when the plants should be fed with a liquid fertilizer once a fortnight. The very long arching leaves should be cleaned regularly, care being taken not to bend the leaflets. If potted on as required, which is usually every other spring, though you may find a vigorous one pushing itself out of its pot in the summer, there should be no trouble with leaf edge scorching. This occurs when the roots are damaged mechanically, by drought or waterlogging, or if the plant is left in a draught.

Do not put a howea into a bottle garden in mistake for *Neanthe bella*, for it grows too fast.

Hoya spp.

There are two species of hoya, the wax flower, sometimes used as house plants. The easiest to manage are the variegated forms of *Hoya carnosa* which is a climber that needs some sort of frame for training. The type has deep reddish–brown stems and fine thick, deep green evergreen leaves, but the others have cream at the edge *(variegata)*, or cream in the centre *(exotica)*.

You will probably be worried when this plant produces long bare stems, but if you resist the temptation to prune them off many will then produce curious knobs. Left alone each knob will develop a lovely hanging cluster of pale pink, scented, waxy flowers at any time during the summer, and not until after this will it grow any leaves. The old knobs will produce more flowers the next year, so do not tidy these up either or you will lose next years crop.

Hoya bella is a very lax grower, almost a trailer, which is apt to rot off at the roots if overwatered, and is therefore sometimes sold grafted on to *H. carnosa*. It looks well on a plant pole or can be stood up on an inverted pot to raise it off a table, for the growths are not very long. Its leaves are small and greyish green, but the flowers, which occur at the ends of the numerous side shoots, are white with pink centres, and smell marvellous. It needs a temperature of 16°C (60°F), whereas *H. carnosa* will survive in a minimum temperature of 10°C (50°F).

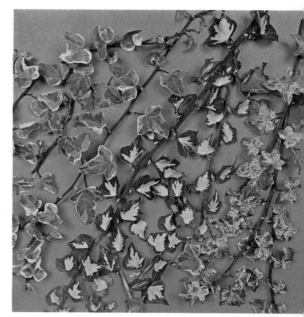

Three varieties of *Hedera helix*: left to right; Glacier, Jubilee, *lutzii*

Hedera helix Buttercup

Hypocyrta glabra

The clog plant, so called from the shape of its little orange flowers, is most worth growing for its excellent deep green shining leaves. It needs a minimum winter temperature of 10°C (50°F) and must then be kept only just moist. In spring and summer when growing fast give more water and liquid fertilizer, but ensure that the pot drainage is good. It will grow in a peat mix. It branches freely and can be encouraged to do so by pinching out the shoot tips, but whatever you do it will turn from a small bushy habit to a sprawler or trailer, so its best place is on a plant pole or where it can hang over a stand edge. It enjoys full sun, and the brighter the light the less leggy it will become, and the more flowers will be formed. Replace every few years.

Maranta leuconeura

Most plants cultivated under the name maranta are actually calathea (see page 30) and all marantas have to be treated as recommended there. The best is probably *Maranta leuconeura*, with leaves in shades of green and either green or purple below. The leaves close together in pairs at night, giving it the name prayer plant. It has a very good variety, *M. l. erythrophylla*, which is sometimes called *M. tricolor*, in which the veins on top as well as those on the back are red. These plants make good wide clumps and look best in half pots (azalea pots).

Monstera deliciosa

This is a once–seen–never–forgotten plant, with leaves gashed and holed in a most surprising manner. The older the plant gets the more complicated this becomes and it is fun to watch the huge leaves (curled up like any other arum) unroll. Monstera is not a difficult plant if you have the right place and temperature for it (18°C, 65°F). It does its rapid best to turn into a climber and produces long aerial roots as it goes, which in the wild would be taking in tropical rain. If you can provide any support system which you can cover with sphagnum moss and keep moist these roots will grow into it and grow all the faster, but they will put up with just dangling. The amount of water needed in the big pot when the plant is in full growth is great, but do not let water lie around the collar. You know when you have been giving enough for sap will then drip from the ends of the leaves, so keep clear of wooden furniture and floors or the polish will be gone. Give liquid feed only occasionally unless you can stand the plant in a great staircase well where it can ascend to a fair height.

Maranta leuconeura

Left and right
Hibiscus rosa-sinensis comes in a variety of colours

Monstera deliciosa (back) *Asplenium nidus*
(right) *Dracaena marginata concinna* (left)
and *Hedera helix* Glacier (front)

Right
Left to right: *Chlorophytum comosum
variegatum* (in trough), *Heptapleurum
arboricola* and *Sansevieria trifasciata laurentii*

Neanthe bella

The plant sold under this name is a slow–growing palm and a tiny plant of it is just right for giving height in a bottle garden. It does well in rooms, however, if kept among other plants so that the air is not too dry. It does not want more than a moist soil, only occasional feeding and preferably some shade. The winter minimum temperature should be 10°C (50°F).

Neoregelia spp.

A bromeliad genus which differs from aechmea and billbergia in that its flowers are stemless in the centre of the false rosette, looking like eggs in a nest. It was once part of the genus *Nidularium*.

The fleshy, strap–shaped leaves do not always form a 'vase'; they are frequently coloured both at the tips and towards the centre of the plant, especially at the time of flowering, when the bracts and flowers may form a vivid contrast. Because of this habit it is best to keep neoregelia below eye level, on low stands or on the outskirts of groups at floor level. The pots must contain a well–drained, peaty soil mix, and the plants can be watered from above into the centre of the leaves. The best colours and most regular flowering occur if the plants can be kept in a good light with some sun. They will grow at most temperatures down to 7°C (45°F).

Nephrolepis spp.

Nephrolepis exaltata is variously called the ladder fern, sword fern, Boston fern, feather or lace fern and has innumerable varieties, many of which have been popular as house plants for generations. Provided it can be kept out of direct sunlight and in reasonably moist air, as when surrounded by moist peat, the less intricately divided forms often do well. The more the fronds are subdivided, and *N. exaltata* runs to some fantastic lace–like forms, the more they resent dry or draughty air, and yet appreciate higher temperatures, 10 to 13°C (50 to 55°F).

They soon get too big for most indoor protection and you will have to rely on daily misting with tepid water around the plants to keep the air moist. Do not soak the finely cut leaves. The soil needs to be very peaty, but well drained, and must never be allowed to dry out.

Nephrolepis cordifolia has less divided leaves than most varieties of *N. exaltata*, and makes a good house plant.

Top
Neanthe bella (left) and *aphelandra* (right)

Bottom
Nephrolepis exaltata

Right
Neoregelia carolinae tricolor (red, yellow and green) and *Nidularium fulgens* (red and green)

Nidularium spp.

These are the plants closely related to neoregelia (see page 54), but in which the coloured (red and orange) floral bracts grow out to form a centre piece with the blue or white flowers tucked in among them. The true leaves may be flecked with dark on light green *(Nidularium fulgens)* or bronze on green *(N. innocentii)*, but are not parti–coloured as in neoregelia, though *N. innocentii striatum* has longitudinal yellow stripes. Grow as neoregelia, below eye level.

Pandanus spp.

Do not attempt to grow these screw pines unless you have a well–heated room, for they like a growing temperature of 18 to 21°C (65 to 70°F). But given that and a certainty that no emergency will bring it below 13°C (55°F) they make interesting foliage plants with saw–edged variegated leaves rather like a pineapple, arranged in spirals so that when they

fall the trunk gives the illusion of a screw thread. The overall effect is of a cordyline.

The variegation is either fine yellow longitudinal stripes as in *Pandanus sanderi*, or white, mainly marginal stripes in *P. veitchii*. The brighter the light the better the variegation. As might be expected, at so high a temperature they need plenty of water when growing, but as the leaves come right down the stem when the plants are young, be careful to water only the soil, for the lower leaves sometimes rot if water lodges between the leaf and the stem. At the first sign of such a disaster remove the leaf carefully and dust the stem with diazinon or flowers of sulphur to stop the rot spreading or you will have lost the plant.

Feed only when growing actively, and pot on in peat mix as necessary. Fortunately in pots they do not attain their wild tree heights; 76cm (2½ft) is probably the maximum.

Peperomia spp.
So many species of peperomia suitable for use as house plants have been discovered very recently that it is hard to know them all. Many are especially good in bottle gardens, domes and other moist air situations, but some will withstand less sheltered conditions. The easiest way to choose is to visit a grower. Their rather sappy leaves differ greatly and include smooth–surfaced ones such as *Peperomia magnoliaefolia* (usually seen in its cream–variegated form), deeply ridged ones as in *P. caperata*, and finely marbled ones as in *P. argyreia* (often listed as *P. sandersii*). Most form compact little plants, but *P. scandens* produces trailing stems, and *P. rotundifolia* puts up quite tall branching flower heads, unlike most which produce simple spikes of minute white flowers. *P. caperata* is the best in flower. For bottle gardens select one noted for its foliage and less likely to flower during its three–year period in the bottle, for dead flowers will have to be removed.

Most peperomias have very poorly developed root systems, which are quite adequate for the mossy banks in which they live under tropical trees. They need a little peat mix in small pots, and in these they will overhang the edges, making it impossible to water from above. In fact, watering is the trickest part of their culture, for they need good drainage and succumb to waterlogging. In mixed bowls do not put them with calatheas or other plants which like a moisture–holding soil mix.

Peperomias do best in a minimum temperature of 13°C (55°F), out of draughts and fumes, and in partial shade.

Opposite, top
Peperomia caperata

Opposite, bottom
Left to right: *Howea fosteriana, Beloperone guttata* and *Peperomia magnoliaefolia*

Hoya carnosa exotica (see p. 49)

Top
Peperomia argyreia

Bottom
Pleomele reflexa

Philodendron spp.

The philodendrons include some very good house plants. The best known is *Philodendron scandens*, which climbs, and as it produces aerial roots (similar to but not as strong as those of its relative monstera) it is best given a sphagnum–filled column of plastic netting to cover and root into. It can, however, be trained up canes. The young leaves often show a red tinge and red and purple often occur as stem, leaf–back or vein colour in philodendrons, the darkest being the climber *P. erubescens*. *P.* Burgundy is one of its hybrids.

The leaves of *P. scandens* are comparatively small and heart shaped, but many, such as the climbers *P. sagittifolium* and *P. hastatum*, have much larger, more arrow–shaped leaves similar to their relatives the arums.

Philodendron selloum, which does not climb, has leaves which gradually get more indented the older the plant becomes, as with monstera. In *P. bipinnatifidum* the leaves are doubly divided. This is another bushy form.

All need a minimum winter temperature of 13°C (55°F), a soil mix containing peat, and a reliable supply of water. They are tolerant of shade, smoke and paraffin fumes. Their leaves benefit from syringing or sponging, and the climbers can be pinched out at any stage to keep them in control and make them more bushy. Feed with liquid fertilizer occasionally when growing fast, but do not repot too often for they do well in quite small pots.

Pilea spp.

These are small foliage plants often used in mixed groups. The best, *Pilea cadierei nana*, is a dwarf form of the aluminium plant, in which the leaves arise from soil level and, provided the plant is well fed, have a silvery sheen caused by air below the surface. The other species sometimes met with is *P. microphylla*, called the artillery plant because its insignificant flowers explode puffs of pollen, but of most use because its small leaves have a look of fern about them.

They need rich soil, are not fussy as to light and need plenty of water carefully given. Do not let the temperature fall below 7°C (45°F) and keep well pinched to encourage the plants to branch.

Philodendron bipinnatifidum

Platycerium bifurcatum

This is the stag's horn fern, which does rather better if you take it from its pot, bind it round the rooting area with sphagnum moss and wire it (plastic–covered wire is best) to a suitable block of wood or cork which can be attached by a back fixing to a hook on the wall, or hung on a plant pole. Water it by dipping the block in the sink as necessary—often daily in summer, weekly in winter—drain it and rehang. Try the tiled kitchen or bathroom wall if you are worried about the odd drip.

In a pot it is sometimes difficult to water or even spray without getting small pools of water lodged on the central, almost circular frond, which may envelop the top of the pot, and if left there such water will frequently cause rotting. These fronds grow sideways on, and as they grow they produce the large antler–like fronds.

Feed very occasionally with very weak liquid fertilizer or foliar feed. The minimum winter temperature required is 10°C (50°F).

Pleomele reflexa

This is a close relative of the dracaenas, and has striped yellow and green leaves which form a marked spiral. Treat as recommended for the less tender dracaenas, taking care that only the soil is watered and not the basal leaves, as it grows very slowly and is spoilt by a bare base.

Pteris spp.

This is a genus of mainly tropical evergreen ferns, four species of which are commonly cultivated. The most widely grown are the many varieties of *Pteris cretica*, known as the ribbon ferns. Most of the variations take the form of a heavy subdivision of the edges or ends of the fronds, which are then known as 'crested'; but a pale, silvery–white variation occurs in *P. cretica albo–lineata*.

Other species are *P. argyraea*, where the frond is pinnately divided and the centre of each is much paler; *P. ensiformis*, in which the fertile fronds are upright and the rest pendent (usually grown in its variegated form *victoriae*), and *P. tremula*, where the fronds are bipinnate near the tips but tripinnate near the base.

The smaller plants can be put in bottle gardens, but many grow to 45cm (1½ft) and are best in Wardian cases or plant cabinets where the air is humid, or in any shady situation in which they can be misted and where the minimum temperature is 13°C (55°F), though some forms of *P. cretica* and *P. tremula* will live down to 7°C (45°F) if acclimatized.

Grow in a peat mix in half pots which give room for the rhizomes to spread outwards.

Rhipsalidopsis gaertneri

The Easter/Whitsun cactus was formerly known as *Schlumbergera gaertneri*. It has dark green flattened stems, occasionally three sided, and with not quite such a pendulous habit as *Schlumbergera buckleyi*, the Christmas cactus. The flowers are produced on the ends of the branches in spring and early summer, and are scarlet and without the marked tubular shape of the Christmas cactus.

Coming from humid forest conditions it needs occasional spraying during the summer when it benefits from being in partial shade among other plants. The soil mix must be very free draining. Rhipsalidopsis will stand lower temperatures (10°C, 50°F) than the Christmas cactus.

Rhoeo discolor

This is a relation of zebrina, but making a large, extended rosette of 30-cm (1–ft)-long strap–shaped leaves, deep green above (striped with yellow in variety *vittata*) and purple beneath. It needs a winter temperature of 10°C (50°F) minimum, a peat mix, fortnightly liquid feed during the summer, and care should be taken to water the soil rather than the basal leaves. Its colour is best in good diffused light, but it will grow in shade.

Discard after about three years as the lower leaves become damaged. Offsets can be removed to make fresh plants.

Opposite, top
Rhoeo discolor

Opposite, bottom
A cristate form of *Pteris cretica*

Bottom
Schlumbergera buckleyi

Rhoicissus rhomboidea

This grape ivy is very similar to *Cissus antarctica*, but it is from Natal, and slightly hardier. It has deep green tripartite leaves which are covered with golden hairs when first unfolding; it also climbs by tendrils. It prefers not to be too hot, expecially in summer, needs good indirect light, and will tolerate smoke and fumes better than most house plants. Water sparingly in winter, moderately at other times and spray the leaves occasionally where this can be managed. It needs feeding fortnightly with liquid fertilizer when growing rapidly.

Saintpaulia ionantha

The African violet is probably the most popular flowering house plant, and deservedly so, as it flowers almost all the year, and has a fine range of colours, deep violet, purple, carmine, pink, pale lavender and white, in single and double flowers and with neat green or bronzy foliage. It needs a warm room (10 to 16°C, 50 to 60°F minimum), fairly humid air, a peat mix which should be moist but never waterlogged, and good but diffused light.

It grows to perfection in plastic domes and plant cabinets where the humidity is good and dead flowers can be removed, but will also do excellently if the pots are on sand trays or embedded in moist peat.

Watering from below is much easier and safer than from above as it is important not to wet the leaves or crown. Feed occasionally while in growth. If a leaf stem rots it must

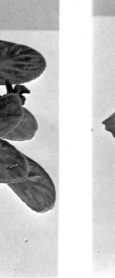

Saintpaulia ionantha can be obtained in a very wide range of colours and forms

be removed right back to the crown, and dead flower stems must also be pulled out completely.

Saintpaulias grow easily from leaf cuttings, but older plants can often be divided in the normal way.

Sansevieria trifasciata

The mother–in–law's tongue, *Sansevieria trifasciata laurentii*, with its long, thick, upright, variegated leaves is one of the most adaptable of house plants, and almost a necessity by reason of its shape which provides a foil for so many of the plants with softer outlines. It prefers a potting mix with some loam in it, needs comparatively little water, and although it produces its best yellow/green contrast in bright light it will grow in shade. Winter temperatures of 10°C (50°F) upwards are necessary.

There is another sansevieria available, sometimes listed as a species, sometimes as a variety of *S. trifasciata*. It is called *hahnii* and comes in two forms, green with irregular silver bandings or a yellow–green variant. These differ from *laurentii* in that the much shorter leaves form a rosette, not unlike a bromeliad. Do not water into the centre, however, and never overwater.

Saxifraga stolonifera

This pleasant little herbaceous plant (known also as *S. sarmentosa*) has silver–veined green leaves edged with pink, and the backs are also pink and very hairy. From among the leaves, which all arise from soil level, it produces red runners (like strawberry runners) which soon make tiny plantlets, giving it the name strawberry geranium. These plantlets can either be potted up to produce more plants (mother–of–thousands is another name for this plant) or just be allowed to swing from the pot which is best placed on a plant pole or stand or in a hanging basket.

If given enough light this plant will bloom in spring, producing loose pinkish–white flowers with two petals longer than the others. It should be kept above 7°C (45°F), but never hot, and needs moderate watering and feeding to keep it in a healthy condition.

Schefflera spp.

There are hundreds of scheffleras, mostly tropical and sub–tropical trees and shrubs, of which three are among the more recent recruits to fine foliage house plants. They all have compound leaves, the individual leaflets of which join the leaf stalk like the spokes of an umbrella, though they are not usually identical in length. In *Schefflera actinophylla* (from Australia) the smooth–edged leaflets may be as much as 18cm (7in) long, but in *S. digitata* (from New Zealand) the leaflets are toothed and slightly smaller. The third, *S. venulosa*, is more generally known as *Heptapleurum arboricola* and is dealt with under this heading (see page 46). All have long leaf stalks which carry the bright green, shiny leaflets well clear of the stems.

Schefflera actinophylla will make a fine specimen up to 2m (6ft) and although *S. digitata* can also be kept to a single stem it branches readily if the growing point is rubbed out, or the top pruned off, when it will make a more useful bush.

These two need a minimum winter temperature of 13°C (55°F), grow best at 16 to 18°C (60 to 65°F), and require good diffused light. Turn as necessary to keep shapely. They are not nearly so sensitive to overwatering as their relative dizygotheca, but should not be allowed to dry out or they lose their lower leaves. Adjust the amount of water to the temperature and rate of growth and keep the plant fed while

in active growth. Use JIP.3 for repotting, but there is no need to worry if the plants become a bit pot bound, as this will merely slow growth. These plants are more tolerant to dry air than many house plants, but appreciate the occasional wash or syringe.

Schlumbergera buckleyi
This is the current name of the Christmas cactus, known for years as *Zygocactus truncatus*. It has flattened pendent stems which (given the correct night length) will produce carmine flowers at the ends throughout mid–winter. There are also pink and salmon varieties or hybrids. The flower buds are only formed if the unbroken night length is at least 13 hours, so keep it away from evening lights. The flowers have tiered parts making a tubular bloom. Each flower lasts about 3 or 4 days but they are usually produced in great numbers over several months.

These plants are actually hybrids of two species that grow wild in the forest trees of Brazil where the humidity is high (unusual for cacti) but the drainage is necessarily good. They do well in pots on a plant pole where other plants contribute to the humidity. During growth they need plenty of water, but always with sharp drainage. Before and after flowering the water is best kept at a lower level for about three weeks. Minimum temperature requirement is 13°C (55°F).

Scindapsus aureus
This is a relative of the philodendrons and needs the same treatment as *Philodendron scandens*, including a moss column. The leaves are streaked and marbled with varying amounts of cream or ivory, and in consequence are best in good diffused light. Prune quite hard in spring to encourage new growth. This replaces some of the old which can become rather straggly.

Top
Setcreasea purpurea

Opposite
Stephanotis floribunda

Setcreasea purpurea

This is like a completely purple zebrina, but with upright stems. It is often called purple heart, and is a good colour foil among tradescantias. It can be grown in any peat mix. If allowed to get too tall it may flop over, but such stems are best pinched out, which will cause the plant to send up fresh new shoots. Keep well watered and at temperatures above 7°C (45°F).

Stephanotis floribunda

This is an evergreen climber with shining deep green leaves and very sweet–scented white flowers produced in clusters along the stems from spring to autumn. When purchased the stem will have been coiled round fine bamboo or wire supports and any further shoots will have to be carefully trained in or shortened, according to their strength and position.

This is not a difficult plant in a thermostatically controlled centrally heated room, for it needs 18°C (65°F) as a minimum throughout the summer, and even in winter when out of flower it will require a minimum temperature of 13°C (55°F).

Water carefully and spray occasionally with water warmed to room temperature. If your tap water is very limy use distilled water, or the leaves will gradually go yellow and drop. If the pots do not receive enough water (even for a short period) during growth the flower buds will dry up, go brown and drop.

Sometimes stephanotis plants are bought with mealy bugs and scale insects on their stems. To get rid of them give a spray with resmethrin or bioresmethrin in place of water.

The plants can be kept for the following year, but are not always easy to get into flower, as they need good light.

Syagrus weddelliana

Better known as *Cocos weddelliana*, this is one of the smaller palms with arching leaves. If purchased sufficiently young this is a good plant for a bottle garden, where it will grow very slowly and appreciate the humid conditions. Make sure that the plant is free of scale insects by spraying with resmethrin before placing in the bottle. If grown unprotected in a living room pack its pot around with moist peat and water and spray regularly. It prefers a temperature of 16°C (60°F), higher than most of the other palms used as house plants.

Tolmiea menziesii

This is a hardy perennial, but is a useful and entertaining plant for children. It is suitable for any cool or unheated room. Its soft green leaves give rise to little plantlets at the top of the leaf–stalks (hence its common name, the pick–a–back plant), and these can be removed and grown on. Its flowers, rather like those of tiarella, are green.

Pot in any good potting mix and water moderately. It dies down in the winter and should then be kept just moist.

Opposite
Tradescantia fluminensis Quicksilver

Bottom
Tolmiea menziesii

Tradescantia fluminensis

This spiderwort or Wandering Jew is one of the easiest plants to grow, and one of the most useful for providing a trailing cover for plant stands. It is normally used in its variegated forms, either green and cream striped or with the addition of a pink flush. Occasionally some varieties revert to plain green (the wild form) and any such shoots should be cut out at once. Quicksilver does not do this.

Tradescantia will grow in sun or shade, in wet or nearly dry soil, in pots or hanging baskets, or planted out into the peat surrounding choicer plants. Short of being frozen it is not easily killed. It is closely related to zebrina which has purple backs to the leaves.

Vriesia splendens

Vriesias are bromeliads which have well–formed rosettes of strap–shaped leaves that are smooth edged, and usually marked very distinctively with deeper colours. In *Vriesia splendens* this is a deep brown, almost black, on green and the flower spike is practically erect, with an orderly array of scarlet bracts shielding yellow flowers, which has earned its name, flaming sword. Treat like *Aechmea fasciata*, but keep it in shade.

Zebrina pendula

This is closely related to *Tradescantia fluminensis*, and is also known as Wandering Jew. It has similarly striped leaves, but with purple backs. The form *quadricolor* has silvery–white, green and pink stripes. Treat as *Tradescantia fluminensis*.

Zebrina pendula

The guests for a short stay

Described here are those pot plants which one is glad to give house room to for a short time but which are not suitable for growing indoors for long periods. Many are flowering plants and need the best lit positions.

If you acquire plants at times of national festivals such as Christmas, Easter and Mother's Day remember that the growers will have spent months and much ingenuity to get these plants into flower for that particular day. Many of them will have come from brightly lit and well–warmed greenhouses and, if not treated properly by the florist, may already have been checked before they reach your home. So it is essential to give them the best possible conditions from the moment you get them. Look to see if they have been properly watered, and if water is needed give it at room temperature. Drain the pot well, place it in a saucer in a warm room, out of draughts but in a good light. Many plants will have been grown to the limit in as small a pot as possible and should really have been potted on into a larger pot weeks before, but do not be tempted to do that now. The plant has had enough checks already, so wait until it has become acclimatized and then if you intend to keep it for any length of time, repot it.

Most of the plants included here are not suitable for permanent growth in a house because when their flowers are over their foliage is not sufficiently interesting to be worth keeping for that alone. Some of them are annuals or are usually treated as such, for example cinerarias, calceolarias and the primulas, and the true annuals you could not keep if you tried.

Certain plants have a resting stage,

Azalea indica hybrid

as is usual with bulbs. At that stage and for quite long periods before and after flowering they are not worth valuable house space. Although many people do buy dried bulbs and pot them up they need quite different conditions at different stages of growth and a maximum amount of light for a long period. If you can buy them when they have already got to the stage of showing bud this will avoid empty–looking bowls and allow your other plants their share of winter sunlight. The only bulbs that do not look tatty after flowering are the ones whose new leaves come after rather than with or before the flower. It is the joy of the flowers that enables one to put up with a naked–looking bulb.

Azalea indica

Small bushy evergreen shrubs, the varieties of which fall roughly into three groups for forcing for winter and early spring flowering. There are single or trumpet–shaped or more or less double varieties, with white, various pink, salmon, crimson and brick–red flowers.

Buy the plants when in bud and check that the root ball has not dried out and that the roots have not been trimmed to cram them into the pot, as may have happened if the plant has been grown in a bed in the greenhouse, rather than in a pot. Such ill–treated plants may not outlive the flowering period.

Azaleas are best kept in temperatures between 10 and 18°C (50 and 65°F), and besides watering need careful spraying overhead. If grown on after flowering they often make interestingly shaped plants, but need bright sunlight and a humid atmosphere to get the buds to form. Only give liquid feed very sparingly during growth; none during flowering.

Calceolaria hybrids

These are best bought in bud in late spring and early summer and discarded after flowering. The flowers are very showy, pouched, and in a variety of mixtures of yellow and red. Strains vary in height and in size of blooms; the tall varieties need staking. The leaves are very soft and damp off readily if wetted, so plants are best watered from below.

Keep in a good light out of direct sunshine in a temperature of 13°C (55°F). Spray with resmethrin if greenfly or whitefly appear.

Chrysanthemum all–the–year–round varieties

These are special varieties selected because they respond readily to scientifically controlled temperatures and night lengths to produce blooms at given dates throughout the year. Many are also treated with dwarfing hormones so that they never reach their normal height, but make a compact plant for pot growing. They are sold when in bud, several small plants to a pot, in colours ranging through white, pink, salmon, bronze, red, crimson and yellow.

Keep the plants watered thoroughly or they will lose their lower leaves; keep in temperatures between 10 and 18°C (50 and 65°F), and discard after flowering. Control any aphids by spraying with resmethrin.

Chrysanthemum Charm and Cascade

Charm chrysanthemums make good bushy plants that can be used as specimens, for if properly treated they will produce a mass of daisy flowers in late autumn. The rather similar Cascade varieties are looser in habit and are trained on a frame to hang down on one side of the pot, often by as much as 1m (3ft). They can look very fine on a plant stand. Keep well watered and in a good light. The Charm plants must be lit on all sides or turned regularly, but the Cascade must face the source of light. Discard after flowering.

Calceolaria hybrids

Pink and white examples of Charm
Chrysanthemums

Coleus

Because coleus are handsome plants even when very small they can be grown in the house for long periods provided a sufficiently light, warm place is available. They are apt to get grey mould below 10°C (50°F) and burn in very hot sun, but need a good light intensity to develop full colour. The leaves are nettle shaped, variegated in several colours of green, cream, red, crimson, brick red and bronze. The plants should be prevented from flowering by pinching out the flower shoots.

Pinch out the tip of any shoots after the fourth pair of leaves to keep the plant branching. Water freely and feed with dilute liquid fertilizer with a relatively high nitrogen content about once a fortnight, until autumn. Discard when the plants become too big, leggy or mouldy.

Crocus spp.

The most likely crocuses to be found in bud in pots are the large Dutch hybrids, which look well as the flowers spear through the white-striped green leaves. They can be obtained in yellow, purple, white and striped varieties. Keep in a sunny, but relatively cool, position at a temperature of 13°C (55°F) and water moderately. Discard after flowering.

Occasionally, with any luck, a garden centre with unsold corms will plant up some of the tinies. They will not be extra early, but should be well worth obtaining. The best are *Crocus ancyrensis*, with several bright yellow flowers per corm, and *C. chrysanthus*, which has lots of varieties, mostly in pale blues, cream or yellows, 'feathered' in bronze, but any species can be grown.

Keep in a sunny position, but not too warm as they go over very soon in too hot a place. The flowers open almost flat in the sun showing the bright orange stigmata and the lovely markings of the throat. Discard after flowering; the leaves become very long and untidy.

Bottom and opposite
Coleus are available in both mixed and individual colours

Coleus Sunset

Cyclamen *hybrids*

Some of these plants have very beautifully marbled leaves which are decorative enough to merit being grown indoors for their own sake, but it is usually best to select a young plant in bud and then, if desired, keep it on an east or west windowsill through to its next flowering. The plants have beautiful flowers with swept back petals, each bloom on its own stem arising from the tuber. Colours are white, white with crimson throat, pink, mauve, red and crimson. Some petals are picotee edged and others are fimbriated.

Cyclamens need very careful watering, which is best done by standing the pot in water and then draining it within half an hour. Water on the top of the tuber or on the crown may cause decay. Any leaves which die must be removed right from the base: if any of the petiole (leaf stalk) remains it will rot and this may spread to other stems. Keep the plant in a temperature of around 13°C (55°F), not in a hot place.

Water with dilute liquid fertilizer once a fortnight between flowerings, but only when new leaves are being produced in quantity. The tuber grows larger every year and when very big does not give as good results as younger plants. Discard after the third year at the latest.

Cymbidium *hybrids and varieties*

These orchids make very fine house plants when in flower. As they tend to flower only once in two years try to return them to a cool greenhouse between flowerings. They make fine sprays of beautiful, long–lasting blooms during the winter and early spring, do not require a very high temperature (10 to 18°C, 50 to 65°F) and will tolerate fairly low light

intensities. They vary enormously in colour and markings and are best chosen when at least one flower is open. They must never be allowed to become either dry or waterlogged. They need a moist atmosphere.

Erica spp.

Collectively known as winter heaths, the South African erica varieties are greenhouse grown for the Christmas market. *Erica gracilis* has pink and white flowers, *E. nivalis* is very like it but white, and *E. hyemalis* is rosy red. They are grown from cuttings, often lined out in beds in the greenhouse, and then lifted and trimmed to fit the small pots in which they are sent to market. This usually means that the plants barely live to finish their flowering. It is worth paying more if you can be sure that the cutting was rooted into a pot.

They do not need a temperature much above 10°C (50°F), but must be in an airy, well–ventilated and light place. Do not allow the peaty compost to become dried out as it will prove difficult to get it properly wet again.

Euphorbia pulcherrima (Poinsettia)

Poinsettias are grown for the showy bracts in scarlet, pink or white which surround the curious little yellowish flowers. They are put on the market for the Christmas and New Year trade and will have been grown in well–heated greenhouses. As they are very susceptible to chilling the growers often deliver them carefully boxed in temperature–controlled vans, but they may easily be chilled in the shops or on the way home. The Mikkelsen hybrids are dwarf.

They need watering regularly while in bloom, keeping in bright light in a temperature of from 13 to 21°C (55 to 70°F). Discard after flowering.

79

Hippeastrum hybrids

These fine bulbs, sometimes incorrectly called amaryllis, can be obtained in flower (red, pink, orange, white and white throated) at almost any time of the year according to when the huge bulb was started into growth. The largest bulbs often produce more than one flower stem.

Buy from a florist or garden centre when the first bud is just coming out of the bulb, the top of which will be above soil level. At this time the leaves may not be showing, but they usually start into growth while the flower stem is lengthening. They are broad and strap–shaped and eventually very long. A warm room, (13 to 18°C, 55 to 65°F), with good indirect light is needed and watering has to be carefully adjusted to the very rapid growth.

Hippeastrums kept moist never have a resting period. This is inconvenient for the seller and so the practice of withholding water after the leaves have developed well has arisen. The leaves die and are cut off. If you choose to do this, repot at this stage. When the bulb produces its next flower stem, after being watered, the new leaves follow in quick succession. There is no need to dry the plant. If the bulb has been well fed (once a fortnight while any active growth was occurring) it will still produce flower stems, but among older, less aesthetically pleasing leaves.

Hyacinthus hybrids

Hyacinths are among the best of the spring bulbs for flowering indoors. There are the delicate, pale–coloured, early Roman hyacinths with many spikes, and the bigger, more solid Dutch hyacinths in reds, pinks, blues, white and yellows. All are sweetly scented. Because some of the bulbs have been 'prepared', that is ripened at carefully controlled temperatures, these flower from Christmas, before the normal season.

Right and opposite
Dutch hybrid crocuses: Peter Pan (white) and Pickwick (purple and white)

Hyacinths in bud are readily available at florists etc.; but if you wish to grow them from bulbs remember that 10 weeks at 9°C (48°F) or less, in damp peat mix, are essential for 'prepared' bulbs, and 14 weeks for others, before bringing them into warmth.

If you have a window box on a ledge facing north, or a cold dustbin store or garage you may succeed. Cupboards indoors are rarely cold enough.

Pots with drainage holes are essential if rain can reach the plants, as bowls become swamped and the waterlogged roots die. Indoors put the hyacinths in a good light and move the bowl round a quarter turn daily so that all sides are lit equally, or they will grow towards the light and flop over, even pulling out any stakes inserted to hold up the flower stems. Stakes are almost a necessity in dull winter weather. Curving flower stalks and green or brown florets at the top of the stalks are more likely to be the result of incorrect treatment in store than subsequent mismanagement, so it pays to buy the best. Discard after flowering.

Left
Crocus ancyrensis

Hydrangea hortensis

Hydrangeas are hardy shrubs, young
plants of which are forced into flower
for selling from late spring to early
summer. Their big heads of blue,
pink or white flowers (really masses
of bracts) are long lasting. If the
flowers are blue, water with rainwater
or distilled water, or failing these,
with boiled water allowed to cool to
room temperature, or they may lose
their clear colour and become purplish pink. Pink flowers appreciate the
lime normally present in tap water.
Keep out of direct sunshine and water
regularly, as they lose a lot of water
from their big leaves.

It is possible to keep the plants for
another season, but it is inadvisable
as the best flowers are always on one–
year–old plants. They will also have
reverted to their normal summer–
autumn season of flowering.

Hypoestes sanguinolenta

This is a small herbaceous plant
grown for the unusual pink spots in
its green leaves, giving it the name
of polka dot plant. It has pink flower
spikes which can be removed before
or after flowering, as preferred. As it
is quite a quick grower it is usually
out of hand by the end of the year,
even if regularly pinched to keep it
branching, and at that stage it is best
discarded. This plant enjoys temperatures of around 13°C (55°F), and needs
plenty of water and the occasional
feed of liquid fertilizer. It is best kept
in a light place, but out of strong sun.

Impatiens hybrids

These Busy Lizzies were already
popular house plants before it was
realized that they made good half–
hardy bedding plants if treated as
annuals. They are really perennials
and it is the named varieties which
are sold in pots from spring onwards.
They should be kept in a fairly warm
place (10 to 16°C, 50 to 60°F) in good
light, such as an east or west window.
Water regularly, feed once a fortnight
all through the summer and pinch out
side shoots to keep the plant bushy.
Pot on regularly as the roots fill the
pot into any good soil mix, loam or
peat based, for example JIP.2, and
they will then keep flowering right
into the autumn. They can be overwintered, but better quality plants are
one year old.

Iris spp.

The small–flowered, bulbous irises
make welcome spring pot plants, but
they are not reliably obtainable from
florists. The species available are *Iris
danfordiae*, yellow; *I. histrio* and *I.
histrioides*, cobalt blue, and *I. reticulata*, which has several named varieties varying in colour from plum
purple and violet to pale blue. These
are sometimes put into pots by garden
centres, who sensibly use up all unsold bulbs, so this is the best place
to look for them. Buy as the buds
are just piercing the soil. The flowers
do not last many days, but they are
very lovely to have close at hand.
Some are faintly scented and all are
beautifully marked. The leaves follow
or are just emerging at the time of
flowering.

Keep cool at 10 to 13°C (50 to 55°F) and in good light, but not in direct sunlight. Water carefully without wetting the flowers and discard after flowering.

Because the flowers come first without waiting for the leaves to grow you do not have to keep these plants in your best positions trying to get a good display of leaves before the flowers emerge. So provided you can start their roots growing in a cold cupboard (at about 7°C, 45°F) until the buds start to push up you can grow them from small bulbs quite successfully. Plant in autumn in half pots rather than bulb bowls, and only keep just moist until obviously shooting up. Watch out for aphids for they sometimes hatch from eggs laid on last year's bulb scales.

Top
Cymbidium Ranjeta (see p. 78)

Bottom
If cymbidiums are purchased when the flower spike is still green much enjoyment will be obtained from watching each bloom develop until the spike is a trail of colour

Kalanchoe blossfeldiana

These South African plants with shiny succulent leaves are another species taken in hand by growers who provide long night treatment to get them in flower at almost any time of the year. The commonest form has brilliant scarlet flowers, but others have orange or yellow. Some strains grow up to 45cm (18in), but the neatest are only about 20cm (8in). They should be kept on the windowsill in good light and will survive a minimum temperature of 7°C (45°F), but respond well to higher temperatures. Water regularly at all times and keep in the smallest pots possible as the plants flower best when their roots are restricted, and if fed fortnightly with a high potash fertilizer (such as the liquid feed given to tomatoes) will go on flowering for months on end. They are best discarded when they have finished flowering, but they will last for years, flowering at their natural time of late winter and early spring.

Narcissus spp. and hybrids

Narcissi (and this name includes the daffodils) are not outstandingly good pot plants. They grow too much leaf and are too tall. The florists usually have a very restricted range of daffodils in pots, often only the early trumpet variety forced in time for Christmas. Although almost any kind is welcome, it is still a pity that growers are not more enterprising and do not try some of the shorter–stemmed hybrids and more of the sweet–scented *tazetta* hybrids which last so well.

There are two varieties which can be had in flower before the winter cold treatment needed to start other kinds into growth, and as they are in flower within eight to ten weeks of being started, I consider them well worth the effort. They are *Narcissus* Scilly White (or Paper White, which is almost identical) and Soleil d'Or. Both should be planted as soon as they are available in the late summer and will then flower from November. The heads carry many small, sweetly scented flowers, yellow and gold in Soleil d'Or. Kept cool at between 10 to 13°C (50 to 55°F) the plants will still be blooming six weeks after their first lovely scent greets you. Plant in peat mix 15cm (6in) or larger pots, rather than in bowls. Water freely once the foliage is showing, and place in a light position, but do not keep the pots in the sun once the flowers are showing. Stake if necessary. Discard when flowering is over.

Much easier to cope with in the house because of their small size are the late winter *Narcissus cyclamineus* and *N. bulbocodium*. They need the traditional cold treatment of 12–14 weeks at 9°C (48°F) or less to start root growth and good light in 15°C (60°F) afterwards. Grow in half pots in peat mix. *N. triandrus albus*, known as angel's tears and flowering in early spring, is rather taller, but not as tall as some *cyclamineus* hybrids, which should be avoided. It is the tiny 15–cm (6–in) ones you need. Later there are *N. canaliculatus* and *N. jonquilla*, which is very sweetly scented. Water regularly once growth starts and plentifully as the buds appear.

Bottom
Impatiens Harlequin Orange

Left
Hippeastrum hybrid

Paphiopedilum insigne

Often called cypripedium or the slipper orchid, these make interesting pot plants as their green and yellow flowers, often marked with brown, are produced in winter or early spring and last well. *Paphiopedilum insigne* is about 30cm (1ft) high and easier than its taller hybrids, which have more variety of flower colour, often being marked with white and bronze and usually having larger flowers. They also require a temperature of 16°C (60°F), whereas *P. insigne* does well at 10°C (50°F) as a minimum. The bigger ones prefer Wardian case treatment, but *P. insigne* will do well in any group of plants needing humid conditions. The compost of peat and loam mix must be kept well watered but never be waterlogged. As they do not die down at any season they can be kept among other mixed foliage plants.

Bottom
Iris reticulata

Pelargonium *varieties*

The well known 'geraniums' have been grown in cottage windows for generations. There are three main flowering types: the regal, with soft leaves and large, rather loose heads of bicolour flowers, mainly in shades of pink, produced in early summer; the zonal–leaved, with a coloured zone on the leaves, and which have closer, more pronounced heads of single or double flowers in scarlet, pink or white, appearing all the summer; and, best beloved, the ivy-leaved pelargoniums, flowering for eight months of the year, with shining, light green leaves and pale pink flowers in heads and a sprawling habit which enables the plants to be trained up or down or along the edge of a container.

Some forms closely related to the ivy–leaved pelargoniums have the veins marked out in white and can be used as foliage plants. There are also scented–leaved varieties, the in-significant flowers of which are best removed. They have very varied leaves with many distinct scents, and are best placed where they can be brushed against or handled.

All need good light, an airy situation and plenty of water during the growing season and a temperature of around 13°C (55°F). Feed with liquid fertilizer once every 14 days whilst new growth is being made. Pelargoniums can be stored almost dry during the winter at a temperature of 4 to 7°C (40 to 45°F) if so desired.

Primula spp.

Four winter–flowering primulas, are all grown for flowering indoors in good light. The best show is obtained from *Primula malacoides* which makes many spikes of small pink, mauve, lavender, crimson or white flowers. It is discarded as soon as it has finished flowering. *P. obconica* has slightly larger, looser spikes of bigger flowers, usually in softer shades of the same

colours. They do not stand so clear of the leaves and are not all produced at once, but may continue to be formed occasionally during the spring and summer. *P. kewensis* is bright yellow and sweetly scented and will last for many years if desired, though the best flowers are always on the younger plants, and they are no great ornament in their resting stage. *P. sinensis* has pleasant foliage and good–sized flowers in many colours, but they do not stand out from the leaves as well as do those of the other species. Discard after flowering.

Primula acaulis, the polyanthus, especially the large–flowered varieties which come in many brilliant colours, also make good pot plants for a short period in early spring. Discard them after flowering. The colours are rarely as bright indoors as out, even in a good light.

All these primulas need airy conditions and a minimum temperature of 10°C (50°F), below which they may be attacked by grey mould. Water carefully from below to prevent collar rot and rotting of the leaf bases. Remove any dying leaf right to the crown.

Some people are allergic to certain primulas, particularly *P. obconica*, coming out in a rash when handling them. This does not happen with the polyanthus, which is the best primula for such people to grow.

Right
Hydrangea hortensis

Senecio hybrid (Cineraria)

Senecio hybrids (Cineraria)

The cinerarias are grown to produce a succession of plants in flower from winter to early spring. There are several types, varying in height and the size of the daisy–like flowers. The colours are usually strong; blue, violet purple, crimson and brick red, often with a white eye. Buy in bud, keep in a temperature of 10 to 18°C (50 to 65°F) for best results and in a good light, but out of direct sunlight. Water from below as the plants are apt to rot off at soil level and wetted leaves usually decay. If the plant flags unpot and look for root aphis, unless flagging is obviously due to under-watering; burn the plant and check other pots in the vicinity should they be present. If the roots are dead the probable cause is overwatering, drowning the roots. Discard after flowering.

Sinningia (Gloxinia)

These tuberous–rooted plants have very handsome velvety leaves and large, trumpet–shaped flowers which are usually in rich, deep colours; reds, blues and violets, sometimes with a white throat. They flower from mid–summer to autumn according to when the tuber was planted or the seed was sown.

They are best bought when about to flower. The plants need a temperature of at least 16 to 18°C (60 to 65°F) and good indirect light. Water very carefully, avoiding spilling water on the leaves or the tubers, but make sure that the air is kept humid round the plants by packing moist peat round the pots.

Gloxinias should be grown in peat mix and fed regularly with dilute liquid fertilizer once a fortnight until the late autumn if the tubers are to be kept. They have to be stored in warmth and when restarted into growth they will need good light and attention which you may think would be better given to other plants.

Top
Narcissus bulbocodium

Bottom
Narcissus Paper White

Solanum capsicastrum

These small shrubs are valued for their cherry–sized berries, which are orange–scarlet in mid–winter, giving the plant the name winter cherry. They are best in a minimum winter temperature of 10°C (50°F), but do not put them in too hot or dry a place as the berries will then wrinkle quickly. Keep watered regularly and, if you propose to keep the plant, feed occasionally with liquid fertilizer or the leaves become grey green and may drop instead of remaining evergreen. Indoors it is sometimes difficult to get enough of the small white flowers to form. They should be hand pollinated or sprayed with a tomato setting compound. The young berries are a pleasing light green.

Streptocarpus hybrids

The new hybrid streptocarpus raised by the John Innes Institute have provided a new race of free–flowering house plants for people who would have had poor results with the older kinds. The dainty, funnel–shaped flowers are produced all the summer, and can be obtained in named varieties of various colours, lavender, vio-let, cerise and pink. The plants need a warm room (16°C, 60°F), plenty of water and a humid atmosphere, but do not want direct sunlight. They are showy subjects for a plant cabinet used as a room divider, though such protection is not essential for these modern hybrids, or they can be kept on the edge of other groups which help to maintain the humidity.

Tulipa varieties

On the whole tulips do not make very good pot plants because so many are too long stemmed, and among the short ones some form rosettes of leaves which make them unsuitable for growing close together in pots. Growers force many of the naturally early spring dwarf singles and doubles and a few Darwin varieties to bring them into flower by mid–winter. They like long stems for cutting. Heights range from 20 to 45cm (8 to 18in). The taller ones need careful staking. Buy in bud and keep in a cool place, 10 to 13°C (50 to 55°F), and out of direct sunshine, for they do not last very long in flower in heat. Keep well watered with tepid water. Discard after flowering.

Top left
Zonal pelargonium Lady Alice

Top right
Zonal pelargonium Frank Headley

Bottom left
Paphiopedilum insigne

Bottom right
Regal pelargonium Grandma Fischer

Top
Senecio hybrid (Cineraria)

Bottom
Streptocarpus hybrid

Opposite
Primula obconica

Tulipa Orange Beauty

Opposite
Sinningia hybrid

94